What Is at Stake Now

Mikhail Gorbachev

What Is at Stake Now

My Appeal for Peace and Freedom

Translated by Jessica Spengler

polity

Originally published in German as *WAS JETZT AUF DEM SPIEL STEHT. Mein Aufruf für Frieden und Freiheit*, by Mikhail Gorbachev ©2019 by Siedler Verlag, a division of Verlagsgruppe Random House GmbH, München, Germany.

This English edition © 2020 by Polity Press
Paperback edition published in 2021 by Polity Press

Reprinted 2022 (twice)

Polity Press
65 Bridge Street
Cambridge CB2 1UR, UK

Polity Press
101 Station Landing
Suite 300
Medford, MA 02155, USA

ISBN-13: 978-1-5095-4321-2
ISBN-13: 978-1-5095-4322-9 (pb)

A catalogue record for this book is available from the British Library.

Library of Congress Cataloging-in-Publication Data
Names: Gorbachev, Mikhail Sergeevich, 1931- author.
Title: What is at stake now : my appeal for peace and freedom / Mikhail Gorbachev ; translated by Jessica Spengler.
Other titles: Was jetzt auf dem Spiel steht. English
Description: Cambridge, UK ; Medford, MA : Polity, 2020. | Includes bibliographical references and index. | Summary: "A major new statement on the key challenges of global politics by one of the greatest statesmen of our time"-- Provided by publisher.
Identifiers: LCCN 2020006726 (print) | LCCN 2020006727 (ebook) | ISBN 9781509543212 (hardback) | ISBN 9781509543236 (epub)
Subjects: LCSH: Globalization. | International relations. | International cooperation. | World politics--21st century. | Liberty. | Security, International.
Classification: LCC JZ1319 .G6713 2020 (print) | LCC JZ1319 (ebook) | DDC 327--dc23
LC record available at https://lccn.loc.gov/2020006726
LC ebook record available at https://lccn.loc.gov/2020006727

Typeset in 10.75 on 14pt Janson Text Lt Pro
by Fakenham Prepress Solutions, Fakenham, Norfolk NR21 8NL
Printed and bound by CPI Group (UK) Ltd, Croydon, CR0 4YY

The publisher has used its best endeavours to ensure that the URLs for external websites referred to in this book are correct and active at the time of going to press. However, the publisher has no responsibility for the websites and can make no guarantee that a site will remain live or that the content is or will remain appropriate.

Every effort has been made to trace all copyright holders, but if any have been overlooked the publisher will be pleased to include any necessary credits in any subsequent reprint or edition.

For further information on Polity, visit our website:
politybooks.com

Contents

Preface

This book is called *What Is at Stake Now* and it deals with nothing less than the future of the global world. Is that not presumptuous? After all, who can say where humanity is heading?

The predictions made one hundred or even just twenty years ago may elicit nothing but smiles of bewilderment today. But I do not want to make any predictions in this book. Instead, I want to reflect on how we are behaving today, what we are striving for and what we should avoid if we hope to preserve our world for future generations.

I am very concerned by the current events, developments and plans of which I have recently become aware.

In January 2020, the *Bulletin of the Atomic Scientists*, which is published in Chicago and has gauged the danger of nuclear war since 1945, moved the hands of the Doomsday Clock ahead by nearly half a minute. Symbolically speaking, it is now 100 seconds to midnight – we are 100 seconds away from war. The situation has not been this dire since 1953.

We live in a globalized world, but we have not yet understood it or learned how to get along together in it. This realization has occupied me for a long time. We often do not notice the dangers lying in wait for us until it is too late. And when we do finally recognize them, we do not dare to act.

We have not learned the art of partnership and cooperation, and politics often lags behind the rapid changes in the world.

I was politically active at a time when my country and the whole world were ripe for colossal changes. We took on the challenges. We made mistakes and misjudged some things. Yet we initiated changes of historic dimensions, and they were peaceful. I think this gives me the right to reflect on the future, too, and to share my thoughts with you, dear readers.

I hope this book inspires you to think and act yourselves – because, ultimately, all of us together are responsible for the future of the global world.

Part I

Our Shared Security

The Militarization of World Politics

World politics is moving in an extremely dangerous direction. Militaristic and destructive tendencies are on the rise. The system for nuclear arms limitation is being dismantled. The decision of the United States to withdraw from the Intermediate-Range Nuclear Forces (INF) Treaty on the elimination of intermediate- and shorter-range missiles was a major blow to the world's security.

The INF Treaty, the Strategic Arms Reduction Treaty (START I) for reducing strategic nuclear weapons and the initiatives of the presidents of the USSR and the USA for eliminating tactical nuclear weapons made it possible to rid the world of thousands of nuclear weapons that had been amassed during the Cold War.

At our first meeting in Geneva in 1985, Ronald Reagan and I articulated the idea that would later lead to the INF Treaty: 'A nuclear war cannot be won and must never be fought.' At the same time, our two states were revising their military doctrines in order to reduce dependency on nuclear weapons.

Compared with the peak of the Cold War, the number of nuclear weapons in Russia and the USA has shrunk by more than 80 per cent today – a historic achievement.

This process did not apply only to nuclear weapons, however. There was also a convention for the elimination of chemical weapons, and the countries of Eastern and Western Europe agreed to radically reduce their armed forces and military spending. This was the 'peace dividend' reaped above all by Europeans after the end of the Cold War.

Since the mid-1990s, however, a countertendency has emerged: the gradual remilitarization of thought and action, a continual increase in military spending and the dismantling of the arms control system.

Of the three main pillars of global strategic stability – the Anti-Ballistic Missile (ABM) Treaty, the INF Treaty and START I – only the latter remains. But the future of the New START Treaty, signed by Presidents Medvedev and Obama in 2010, is now also being questioned. Judging by statements from representatives of the American administration, it too could soon be history.

Today's military activities have come to resemble preparations for an actual war. Documents published by the Trump administration show that US foreign policy is increasingly being geared towards political, economic and military rivalry all over the world. The goal is to develop new, more flexible nuclear weapons, which simply means continually lowering the threshold for the use of such weapons.

In light of this, Russian President Vladimir Putin announced to the Federal Assembly that Russia is developing a number of new weapons systems. He explained at the same time that Russia was not looking for a new arms race, an attitude that undoubtedly reflects that of the population. In the past, our country never initiated a competition in building up arms. Instead, it was forced to play catch-up, responding to the challenge from the other side. Today, not only Russia but the entire world is facing a new politico-military challenge.

The USA wants to dominate world politics by relying on military superiority. At least, this is the impression one gets from recent events.

In the process, the USA wants to marginalize the United Nations and the Security Council and, in effect, replace them with NATO – a military alliance that is not only enlarging its own territory but that also aims to expand its 'sphere of responsibility' all over the world.

I have never made any secret of my opinion that the decision to expand NATO was a major strategic blunder on the part of the West and a move that tended to destabilize the political and military situation in Europe and beyond its borders. In connection with this, I would like to explain once again how this issue was discussed as the Cold War was coming to an end and what conclusions are to be drawn from that today.

In the years when I was the leader of our country, the issue of NATO was being addressed within the context of German reunification. The prospect of a unified German state joining NATO – an organization born during the Cold War – was viewed with serious misgivings by many in our country. We talked frankly about this with our negotiating partners and proposed possible solutions. After long and hard discussions, we agreed that, as a sovereign state, a unified Germany should decide for itself which organizations and alliances to join. But there was more to our agreements than that.

In the early 1990s, we agreed that the territory of the former German Democratic Republic should be given a special politico-military status. Germany pledged not to station any additional military infrastructure, foreign troops or weapons of mass destruction there. The Germans also pledged to reduce their armed forces by nearly half. Germany has upheld these and other stipulations to this day.

At the same time, the military doctrines of NATO and the Warsaw Pact (which still existed then) were being revised. The plan was to strengthen their political components at the expense of military ones. The member states of NATO and the Warsaw Pact signed an agreement to cut their troop numbers.

Some of my critics reproach me to this day for not having

insisted on a legally binding stipulation that would have prevented NATO from expanding into Eastern Europe in the future. But such a demand would have been absurd, even preposterous, because the Warsaw Pact still existed at the time. We would have been accused of destroying it with our own hands.

We achieved all that we could under the circumstances at the time. Russia was fully entitled to demand that the other side act in accordance not just with the letter, but also the spirit of these agreements and obligations. But the mutual trust that emerged with the end of the Cold War was severely shaken a few years later by NATO's decision to expand to the east. Russia had no option but to draw its own conclusions from that.

What Is at Stake

The INF Treaty, which was of historic importance to world peace, is itself now history – and its demise is the fault of the USA. The same is true of the refusal to ratify the Comprehensive Nuclear-Test-Ban Treaty and the withdrawal from the ABM Treaty for the limitation of missile defence systems.

If the INF Treaty is terminated by either of its two parties, the country in question must provide a notification stating the 'extraordinary events the notifying Party regards as having jeopardized its supreme interests'. The country that takes such a serious step must explain to the world community why it has decided to destroy what has been built to date.

What happened? What threat has prompted the United States – whose military spending is many times higher than that of any competing power – to take this step?

Did the USA inform the UN Security Council, which was created for the purpose of resolving conflicts that threaten peace? It did not. Instead, Russia is being accused of alleged treaty violations that even experts have struggled to understand. This all has the tone of an ultimatum.

The argument put forward by the USA is that other countries – particularly China, Iran and North Korea – also have intermediate-range missiles. But this argument is not convincing. In fact, the United States and Russia together still control more than 90 per cent of the world's existing nuclear weapons. In this sense, our two countries do remain 'superpowers'. The nuclear arsenals of other countries are ten to fifteen times smaller.

If the process of reducing nuclear weapons were to continue, other countries would at some point have to join in, including the United Kingdom, France and China. These three states have repeatedly confirmed their willingness to do so. But how can they be expected to show restraint when one of the superpowers wants to lift the existing limitations and expand its nuclear arsenal?

One has to conclude that the USA has decided to withdraw from the treaty not for the reasons it claims, but for a very different purpose: the pursuit of military superiority and a burning desire to cast off any restrictions on rearmament. 'We have more money than anybody else by far', President Trump has said regarding the arsenal of the USA, 'and we'll build it up until they come to their senses.' Build up the arsenal – why, to what end? To impose the country's will on the world?

This is an illusion. In today's world, it is not possible for a single country to achieve a hegemony. This has recently become clear. Even Washington's most loyal allies are no longer prepared to stand to attention before their big brother.

The current destructive trend can only lead to destabilization and a new arms race. The global situation is becoming ever more chaotic and unpredictable. This, in turn, endangers the security of all states, including that of the USA.

The US president said his country was hoping to conclude a 'new treaty that would be much better'. Let us not be deceived by this, or by the assertion of Secretary of State Mike Pompeo that the USA has 'no plans to immediately start deploying new missiles'. This just means the USA does not yet possess such missiles.

Europeans have not been convinced by these assurances either. They are alarmed, and understandably so. Everyone remembers the early 1980s, when hundreds of missiles were stationed on our continent, Soviet SS-20s on one side, American Pershing and cruise missiles on the other. And everyone knows that a new arms race could be even more dangerous.

I welcomed the European attempts to save the INF Treaty. The European Union called upon the United States to think carefully about what withdrawing from the treaty would mean for its own security, the security of its allies and that of the entire world. German foreign minister Heiko Maas, who warned that terminating the INF Treaty would have 'numerous negative consequences', travelled to Moscow and Washington to mediate. Unfortunately, this was to no avail. It is therefore all the more crucial to continue these efforts, even now that the USA has withdrawn from the treaty and thus practically ensured its demise.

Too much is now at stake.

Opponents of the treaty claim that the world has changed substantially, so the agreement is simply outdated. The former is certainly true, the latter is completely false.

Despite all the changes in the world, we cannot do away with the agreements that laid the foundation for global security after the end of the Cold War. Instead, we must put our entire energy into achieving the most important goal: the total elimination of all nuclear weapons.

Equal Security for All:
The Charter of Paris

In November 1990, I returned home from France, where a historic document had been signed at a meeting of the heads of state and government of Europe, the USA and Canada: the Charter of Paris for a New Europe.

On the flight back to Moscow, I read the document again. This charter was much more than just a political declaration. It was a true manifesto, a commitment not only to the people of Europe, but to the whole world.

In it, the signatories announced that 'the era of confrontation and division of Europe has ended'. From that point on, their relations would be 'founded on respect and co-operation', and they would 'undertake to build, consolidate and strengthen democracy as the only system of government of our nations'.

The countries of Europe and the Americas declared that, in the future, they would pursue shared values: a 'steadfast commitment to democracy based on human rights and fundamental freedoms; prosperity through economic liberty and social justice; and equal security for all our countries'.

Equal security for all – this was the prerequisite for everything else. The charter was absolutely clear on this point: 'With the ending of the division of Europe, we will strive for a new quality in our security relations while fully respecting each other's freedom of choice in that respect. Security is indivisible and the security of every participating State is inseparably linked to that of all the others.'

Most importantly, the signatories went on to say:

> We decide to develop mechanisms for the prevention and
> resolution of conflicts among the participating States. ...
> [W]e will not only seek effective ways of preventing, through
> political means, conflicts which may yet emerge, but also
> define, in conformity with international law, appropriate
> mechanisms for the peaceful resolution of any disputes
> which may arise. Accordingly, we undertake to seek new
> forms of co-operation in this area.

When I look at this document today, I count it among
our greatest achievements, as significant as the agreements
reached at our meetings with US presidents Ronald Reagan
in Reykjavik and George Bush in Malta. It was a step out of
the Cold War and into a peaceful future.

Europe has a special role to play here. This is where world
history was decisively shaped in the twentieth century. This is
where ideologies were born that soon came into conflict with
each other on every continent. This is where matters of war
and peace were decided in the most dramatic way.

In the first half of the twentieth century, Europe experienced the catastrophe of two world wars, the deaths of millions
of people, the devastating effects of totalitarian ideologies and
arbitrary rule, and the destruction of justice and morality.

In the second half of the century, Europe and the whole
world faced colossal new challenges. The ideals of peace
and cooperation that were proclaimed with the founding of
the United Nations remained a distant and, for many, often
unreachable goal. The world split into hostile camps. Since
the emergence of nuclear weapons, the very existence of
humanity has been at stake.

The generation of politicians I belong to was shaped in
the post-war period. Some of us participated in the Second
World War as soldiers, others experienced this terrible

scourge as children or adolescents. The Second World War deeply scarred our souls and taught us to treasure peace.

We began making our way in politics during the Cold War and burgeoning arms race, after a historic opportunity for peace and cooperation had been squandered – partially for objective reasons, partially due to the mistakes of individual statesmen.

At the time, politicians and diplomats were mainly concerned with ensuring that the Cold War did not become a real, 'hot' war. But they failed to prevent an arms race. A breakthrough in our way of thinking was necessary for this – and it actually happened, not overnight but as the result of a long intellectual search on both sides of what was then a divided world.

The end of the Cold War was the product of joint efforts. The leaders of the states that held the fate of the world in their hands demonstrated a sense of responsibility and political will. The tremendous changes that paved the way to freedom and democracy for all the peoples of Europe took place peacefully and without violence.

Peace: Words and Deeds

One of the principles of our new political thinking is that security can never be achieved unilaterally at the expense of others. This was the conviction of the political leadership of the Soviet Union at the time. We proposed agreements to our Western partners that aimed to resolve existing conflicts, while taking the interests of both parties into account.

Another important principle was freedom of choice. In the Soviet Union, we granted this right to the peoples of our vast country, which was made up of many different ethnic groups. People now had the right to freely express their opinion, elect their leaders themselves and establish political parties and associations. At the same time, we could not deny this freedom of choice to the peoples of the countries that had been our allies for decades.

We proved our commitment to this principle in practice. In East Germany and the countries of Central and Eastern Europe, people took to the streets and demanded freedom, and not a single one of the hundreds of thousands of Soviet soldiers who were stationed in these countries left their barracks. The Soviet Union did not stand in the way of the people determining their own fate. There was a revolution in Europe, unprecedented and bloodless.

While not underestimating the role played by the people themselves, I want to add the following: this peaceful revolution and, broadly speaking, the new, democratic Europe would not have been possible without the profound changes that had their beginnings in the Soviet Union with glasnost and perestroika.

The Soviet Union and its successor, Russia, thus had the right to expect that our country's security interests would be taken into account in this new Europe. We viewed the Charter of Paris as the start of a development towards a shared, indivisible security.

What remains of the spirit of the Charter of Paris? It seems to have faded into obscurity in the 1990s. Politicians, government ministers and heads of state did not so much as mention this historic document for years. What has become of the key commitment enshrined within it, namely, to 'develop mechanisms for the prevention and resolution of conflicts among the participating States'? Not a single substantial step was subsequently taken in this direction. Ignoring the commitments of the Charter of Paris was just one symptom of a peculiar disease afflicting the Western political elite in the first decade after the end of the Cold War: triumphalism.

What do I mean by this? Three decades ago, no one

doubted that the end of the Cold War was our mutual victory. It came about through dialogue and negotiations on the most complicated problems of security and disarmament, and through the improvement of bilateral relations. Without all of this, the Cold War and the arms race could have dragged on for several more decades. And who knows where that might have led?

Instead of acknowledging this, the West declared itself the victor. For the West, the Cold War did not come to an end until the Soviet Union did. American leaders attributed this to a policy taken from a position of strength.

They concluded that it was now necessary to further boost their military power, impose their own will and create a unipolar world, an American empire. The consequences are obvious, in the Middle East and North Africa, in Yugoslavia and Ukraine. Even in Europe, the very continent that lived through two world wars! This is inexcusable.

Do Not Give Up!

Is there a way out of this vicious cycle of conflict and war? The biggest mistake now would be to panic and hang our heads. It is critical for us to understand our situation and contemplate specific steps for preventing a new arms race.

What can each of us do? First and foremost, do not remain silent. Sound the alarm and debate with those who ignore the danger. Refute the arguments of all those who view the use of force as a path to peace, particularly those who regard nuclear weapons as the guarantee of peace.

I recall my heated discussions on this topic with Margaret Thatcher, the British prime minister at the time. We argued a great deal and often reached an understanding, but on the nuclear issue she held her ground to the last. It was nuclear weapons, she claimed, that had ensured peace in the second half of the twentieth century. World War III would have broken out otherwise. 'Are you really comfortable sitting on this nuclear powder keg?' I asked. I showed her a diagram with a schematic representation of nuclear arsenals as hundreds of 'cells'. Any one of these 'cells' would have been enough to extinguish human civilization as we know it.

I could not persuade Thatcher back then. But today we hear the same arguments in both the United States and Russia, where, one has to admit, there are quite a few proponents of nuclear weapons. I do not want to place the two countries on the same level, but I am certain they are both capable of guaranteeing their own security without nuclear weapons. They have the necessary resources and technologies.

This is not the only argument for reducing and ultimately completely renouncing nuclear weapons, however.

A Dangerous Myth

Nuclear weapons are like a rifle hanging on the wall in a play. We did not write the play, we are not staging it and we do not know what the author intends. Anyone could take the rifle from the wall at any time.

A nuclear weapon can be set off accidentally as a result of a technical defect or through human or computer error. This particularly worries me. Computers are now used everywhere – in aviation, industry and all sorts of control systems – and accidents caused by faulty computers or electronics happen everywhere as well. Nuclear weapons can be triggered by a false alarm, and the shorter a missile's distance to its target, the greater the likelihood of such an accident. They can also fall into the hands of terrorists. Who knows what other surprises they have in store?

My attitude towards nuclear weapons crystallized early

on, back in the mid-1950s when I was in my home region of Stavropol, where I was working for the Young Communist League and the Party.

One day, we activists were shown a film about civil defence in the event of nuclear war. The film did more than merely present diagrams and charts. It showed actual pictures of real atomic bomb tests. The blast wave that tore a building to pieces, trees that were uprooted and tossed through the air, dead livestock and a black wind – the images were terrifying. The attempt to give viewers the impression that one could survive a nuclear war failed to convince me (I quote: 'You must turn away from the explosion ... lie on the floor ... cover yourself with a white sheet ...'). After the screening, I just said to my colleagues, 'Drape yourself in a white sheet and crawl straight to our Danilovsky cemetery!'

If you believe the myth that nuclear weapons have 'saved the world', may I remind you that, during the Cold War, those same weapons brought the world to the brink of nuclear war at least once?

Recently published documents prove just how close humanity came to the abyss during the Cuban Missile Crisis of 1962. Everything hung by a thread. In the end, the world was saved not by nuclear weapons, but by the prudence of the leaders of the two countries: John F. Kennedy and Nikita Khrushchev.

I am certain that both of them, then and subsequently, thought long and hard and their view of nuclear weapons changed significantly. They stopped praising the atomic bomb in their speeches. They also signed an agreement banning nuclear tests in the atmosphere, in space and under water. This not only slowed the development of weapons technology, it also protected the environment from the deadly substances that are released in atomic explosions.

Just as importantly, these leaders changed their way of thinking. We find evidence of this in Khrushchev's memoirs as well as in Kennedy's public statements. 'What kind of peace do I mean? What kind of peace do we seek?' Kennedy asked in his address at American University in Washington. He answered the question himself: 'Not a *Pax Americana* enforced on the world by American weapons of war ... Genuine peace must be the product of many nations, the sum of many acts.' In this speech, Kennedy no longer spoke of the Soviet Union or Soviet people as the enemy.

I believe there was an opportunity back then to stop the arms race permanently, demilitarize politics and move towards a new thinking. But Kennedy did not have an opportunity to even try putting these ideas into political practice. One year later, a bullet in Dallas ended his life. I personally believe this murder is still unsolved.

Today I sense that the world is facing an acute, totally uncontrolled military and political confrontation between the two leading global powers. All the mechanisms previously put in place to ensure peace have been damaged, weakened or threatened. If things continue like this, a catastrophe could happen. Those pursuing this hellish path should think about it.

We have heard numerous reports lately of dangerous near collisions between military aircraft and navy ships. Does a real collision have to happen before politicians and military officials come to their senses? Do they really not see the danger of a chain reaction of unstoppable events?

Is there a way out of the current situation? Negotiations are the only sensible solution. Every effort must be made to end the mutual accusations, belligerent rhetoric and arms build-up and to start an earnest dialogue.

The Negotiations We Need Now

The negotiations that must – and I believe will – start will be difficult. This is because we face new threats, such as non-nuclear weapons of great precision and long range that blur the line between weapons of mass destruction and conventional weapons. Then there are space weapons and cybertechnology.

All of this must be negotiated. But the main thing is to stop the new nuclear arms race, in which there can be no winners.

In the history of negotiations on the limitation and reduction of nuclear weapons, there were always different periods as well as both successes and setbacks.

Think back to the early 1970s. In an extremely difficult situation, the Soviet Union and the United States entered into negotiations on strategic armament. With the ABM Treaty, they came to an agreement on limiting missile defence systems. This was an important breakthrough, both intellectually and morally.

Politicians and military officials realized that it was impossible to create a reliable missile defence shield, that nothing could provide protection against the devastating consequences of a nuclear war. The deployment of missile defence systems was initially limited to two sites and then reduced to one.

Granted, Ronald Reagan later believed in the effectiveness of missile defence, and the USA withdrew from the ABM Treaty under President George W. Bush. And yet, this treaty had an effect: it prevented an arms race in this area.

In terms of strategic offensive weapons, however, everything turned out much worse. In May 1972, in conjunction with the ABM Treaty, Leonid Brezhnev and Richard Nixon signed an interim agreement to freeze the number of strategic ballistic missile launchers at the maximum limits reached at that point.

This heralded an easing of tension between East and West, and the nuclear arms race appeared to become pointless and impossible. But one aspect remained unaddressed: the ability to equip missiles with multiple independently targeted warheads. Neither side wanted to relinquish this option.

What was this? A cunning move on the part of the military-industrial complex? A sudden technological breakthrough for which the politicians were unprepared? Short-sightedness on their part, or a sheer inability to consider all the consequences of deploying these new weapons?

Perhaps a little of everything. Regardless, the number of warheads on land- and sea-based long-range missiles rose rapidly, and by the end of the 1970s, the size of the world's nuclear arsenals had increased many times over. This continued in the first half of the 1980s. Then there was the problem of intermediate-range missiles, which led to a crisis.

Break the Vicious Cycle

When I rose to the leadership of the USSR and looked into the situation of nuclear disarmament negotiations, I was baffled. Negotiations were taking place, diplomats and military officials were meeting regularly. They gave speeches to each other, hundreds of litres of beverages of various strengths were consumed at receptions, and meanwhile the arms race continued, arsenals increased and nuclear testing carried on. There was a terrible inertia, a vicious cycle it was impossible to escape.

In the second half of the 1980s, the political leadership of both the USSR and the USA came to the realization that all of this could not go on indefinitely. I see here a parallel to the motto of perestroika: 'We can no longer continue to live this way.'

Despite all the differences of opinion in my discussions on specific issues with Ronald Reagan and Secretary of State George Schultz, we agreed that the nuclear arms race not only had to be stopped, it had to be reversed. The breakthrough came in Reykjavik. At the summit in the Icelandic capital in 1986, the foundations were laid for the treaties on strategic and intermediate-range weapons. Nevertheless, the talks occasionally stalled. Without political will, everything could have fallen apart. But in the end, the result was achieved.

This is an important lesson for the present day. We achieved the breakthrough in part because we did not restrict ourselves to discussing ceilings, sub-ceilings or verification problems, regardless of how important they were. We tried to look further than this. We not only declared nuclear war to be unacceptable, we discussed – first on an expert level and then on a political level – the question of how a nuclear war could be prevented.

In June 1990, I visited the United States. The agenda was extensive and complex. We had a difficult discussion of the problems associated with German unification, but in the end reached a common understanding. Equally important was the discussion of nuclear weapons. The pace of the negotiations for reducing strategic offensive arms had slowed, and the future treaty was at risk of getting bogged down in a jumble of technical details. Political impetus was necessary once again, and it came in the form of a joint statement issued by the two presidents.

The joint statement was the first to define strategic stability for the two powers. It said that strategic relations would be pursued to 'remove incentives for a nuclear first strike'. This was an important step towards preventing the first use of nuclear weapons. And it was not just declarative (though declarations are important in politics): it was accompanied by specific guidelines for military policy.

First, the USSR and the USA acknowledged the connection between strategic offensive and defensive weapons. Consequently, missile defence systems should also be subject to limitations and could not be deployed without restrictions. Second, it was noted that stability depended on reducing the concentration of warheads on strategic delivery vehicles. Third, priority would be given to weapons that are more survivable in the event of a military conflict.

On the basis of this agreement, the United States said it was prepared to waive its previous demand that the Soviet Union dismantle its mobile missile systems. All these principles were adopted in START I, which was signed one year later in Moscow and was later ratified and fully implemented by both parties.

Today, new so-called advanced weapons and changes in military doctrines threaten to undermine these principles and thus strategic stability as a whole. Therefore, one of the most important aims of future negotiations should be to strengthen and further develop these principles.

Now is also the time to seriously question the existing military doctrines. The global community has the right to know why the leading nuclear powers have not fundamentally ruled out first use of nuclear weapons. The possibility of responding to a non-nuclear threat with a nuclear strike has always been part of the military doctrine of the United States. This provision has remained unchanged.

Why? Is such a strong military power incapable of guaranteeing its own security without threatening to employ the most destructive weapons in the history of humankind? We have yet to hear a convincing answer to this question.

The military doctrine of the Russian Federation published in 2014 also provides for such an option 'in the event of aggression against the Russian Federation with the use of conventional weapons when the very existence of the state is in jeopardy'. At the same time, President Putin recently declared: 'We have no preventive strike in our concept for the use of nuclear weapons. This means we are only prepared to use nuclear weapons, and we will only do so, if we are certain that someone, a potential aggressor, is conducting a strike against Russia, against our territory.'

If we enter into a discussion on this basis, hopefully we can bring the opposing positions closer together and then move on.

Act as a Role Model

Today, the main responsibility lies with the United States and Russia. These two countries should resume their negotiations, find a way out of the impasse and show the world that they are willing to meet their obligations under the Treaty on the Non-Proliferation of Nuclear Weapons. As a reminder, the central obligation is for the nuclear powers to reduce and ultimately eliminate their own arsenals, in return for the majority of other countries agreeing to renounce nuclear weapons.

At the Review Conference for the treaty in 2015, no consensus was reached, and the non-nuclear states openly expressed their dissatisfaction with the current situation. The next conference is due to take place in 2020. I fear that this time, since the USA has withdrawn from the agreement on scaling down Iran's nuclear programme, we can expect things to fall apart. The consequences would be even more alarming.

We have examples from recent history of nuclear powers acting as role models for others. I am referring not only to the treaties signed at the end of the Cold War, but also to the history of atomic testing. The world breathed a sigh of relief when the USSR, the USA and the UK concluded the treaty in 1963 for banning nuclear tests in the atmosphere, in outer space and under water. Other nuclear states, even those that have not signed this treaty, subsequently followed their example.

Three decades later, the situation virtually repeated itself. The Soviet Union insisted on ending all nuclear testing and declared a moratorium on conducting nuclear explosions. This was not immediately accepted, but we remained persistent. The result was a new treaty that banned all nuclear tests. Although the United States exacerbated the situation by refusing to ratify the treaty, public opinion and common sense ultimately prevailed, and in 1992 the USA conducted its last nuclear test in the Nevada desert. In the twenty-first century to date, only North Korea has tested nuclear weapons. Yet there is reason to hope that it, too, can be convinced to give up its nuclear programme – regardless of how difficult the negotiations may be.

If Russia and the United States sit down at the negotiating table again, the general mood will improve, as will the conditions for dialogue with other countries that also possess nuclear weapons. This dialogue could start with consultations for clarifying mutual intentions, discussing military doctrines, initiating confidence-building measures and ensuring transparency. Then negotiations and the first agreements could follow.

It is difficult to say what these negotiations might look like. Perhaps the first phase of discussion will focus on 'freezing' nuclear arsenals. Since some states have become convinced that their security cannot be guaranteed without nuclear weapons and have shown their teeth, so to say, could they perhaps stop at that?

A few states have voluntarily renounced nuclear weapons, either by destroying the weapons they had previously built (South Africa) or, like Ukraine, Kazakhstan and Belarus, by giving up the weapons they 'inherited' from the USSR.

Experience has shown that competition is possible not only in building up arms, but also in mutual restraint – to be followed by legally binding agreements.

In May 2009, I took part in the opening ceremony of the World Peace Bell Park in Gangwon-do province on the border of the demilitarized zone between North and South Korea. The fiercest battles of the Korean War were fought

In this region in the 1950s. Today there is a peace park with a bell made of melted-down cartridge cases collected from the battlefields of the Korean War and other sites around the world.

During this trip, I sensed how closely military and political factors, history and regional security are intertwined. Literally on the eve of the park's opening, North Korea conducted a nuclear test. It was a provocation. But the park opened and the bell pealed in front of thousands of people who had flocked there from all provinces of South Korea. On this day, I saw how fervently ordinary people long for peace and for the liberation of the Korean peninsula from nuclear weapons.

There is no doubt that the vast majority of people in other parts of the world are also opposed to nuclear weapons. Ultimately, all the states that possess nuclear weapons must sit down at the negotiating table and talk about abolishing them. Non-nuclear states should also participate on an equal footing, because their opinion matters as well.

It is just as important to conduct negotiations for preventing an arms race in areas that are on the brink of a quantum leap, as it is said. This mainly applies to space weapons, information technology and cybertechnology. It is terrible even to contemplate what might happen if the tremendous possibilities of modern technology are put to use for military purposes.

Consultations on this issue should start as soon as possible in the UN Security Council. The danger of the militarization of space and cyberspace is real, and its potential consequences are catastrophic.

We Must Act Together

Of all international security problems, the nuclear threat is the most urgent. It is not the only issue, however. Political processes are constantly subject to spontaneity, haphazardness and unpredictability in various forms.

In some regions – Africa, Southeast Asia, Latin America – the end of the Cold War has made decades-old conflicts a thing of the past. But not everywhere in the world. In many places, conflicts have been 'frozen', although this metaphor is misleading – because conflicts smoulder, flare up from time to time and risk exploding. New conflicts have emerged on top of the old, and it seems that the international community has resigned itself to at least some of them. We must not accept this.

I find myself wondering where to look for solutions, and I always come back to the United Nations, its history and its place in today's world.

I am deeply concerned that the UN might lose its role as the main tool for solving problems of international security. Yet this is precisely what it was created for. It has not always lived up to this mission in its history, but there have been successes.

To this day, everything depends on whether the UN member states can develop the will to cooperate and take multilateral action in order to prevent and resolve conflicts and crisis situations. Accomplishing this depends mainly on whether everyone, particularly its most influential members, demonstrates such a will.

By adopting a joint position and taking joint action, the international community can achieve its goals. A recent example is proof of this.

In the late summer of 1990, a crisis erupted in the Middle East, which, under the conditions of the Cold War, could have led to a confrontation between major powers with unforeseeable consequences. In early August, Iraqi troops marched into Kuwaiti territory. A small Arab state was overrun, and Saddam Hussein's regime announced that the country of Kuwait had ceased to exist.

Right from the start, we viewed this as a serious and unacceptable breach of international law. The vast majority of other nations felt the same way. Nonetheless, the actions of the Iraqi regime posed grave problems for us.

We had a treaty of friendship and cooperation with Iraq. Thousands of our people were in the country at the time, including military experts. We had major economic interests there. The Iraqi regime hoped that if the USSR would not support its actions, it would at least look the other way.

In this situation, we refused to act in accordance with the logic of the Cold War – that is, following the motto of 'He may be a son of a bitch, but he's our son of a bitch'. We immediately told Saddam Hussein that his actions were unacceptable.

For the first time in many years, the USSR and the USA were not on opposite sides of the barricades in a regional conflict. But the question was how we could achieve our desired goal: forcing Iraqi troops to withdraw from Kuwait and restoring Kuwait's sovereignty.

Many in the West, including influential figures in the United States, insisted on using military force as quickly as possible. We, however, thought it was necessary to look for a peaceful way out of this situation. This is exactly what I told President George Bush in early September 1990 at a summit in the Finnish capital of Helsinki.

We agreed to take action via the UN Security Council, which imposed a number of sanctions against Iraq and demanded the immediate withdrawal of Iraqi troops from Kuwait. I can say that our conscience is clear. We did everything possible to achieve this goal by political means through negotiations. I personally took part in hours-long negotiation marathons and telephone calls with the leaders of the United States, Iraq and the Arab countries.

Saddam Hussein remained irrationally obstinate, and it became impossible to avoid the use of military force. By the time Iraq declared its willingness to comply with the provisions of the UN Security Council resolutions, it was far too late – US troops had already entered Kuwaiti territory. Although it was not possible to fully realize the plan for peacefully settling this crisis, the overall outcome was positive. American troops did not cross the border into Iraq, and the United States opted against occupying the country and forcing a 'regime change'.

A Fatal Mistake

The USA behaved very differently during the second Gulf crisis in 2003. This war itself was not inevitable. When the US president decided to use force against Iraq – under the pretence that the country had weapons of mass destruction – he not only disregarded the facts, he also went against the opinion of the vast majority of other countries around the world, including allies of the USA. Above all, he did so without the approval of the United Nations. This was a clear violation of international law.

Right from the start, I said that the US military operation was a mistake – indeed, a strategic mistake. But we could not begin to imagine the scope and consequences of this mistake at the time. These only became apparent in the following years, and they include the growing threat of terrorism around the globe.

Of course, this threat has older causes as well, and every country that is in any way responsible for its creation must acknowledge this. In other words, admit your mistakes and draw the right conclusions from them.

One such mistake was the decision by the Soviet leadership to send troops to Afghanistan in 1979. This decision was made by a small group of people, without thorough analysis and against the advice of experts and even the military leadership. Once we had acknowledged this mistake, we decided to pull the Soviet troops out of Afghanistan. Moreover, the Congress of People's Deputies of the Soviet Union adopted a resolution in 1989 that politically and morally condemned the decision to deploy troops to Afghanistan.

When a deputy to the Russian State Duma recently suggested that this resolution should be declared invalid, I spoke out firmly against his immoral 'initiative' and called upon Russia's leadership to take a stand. Although the Russian president did not publicly comment on the matter, this proposal was not put to a vote. I hope this means the issue is over and done with.

It is important to remember, however, that in the discussions about Afghanistan in the second half of the 1980s, we offered to work together with the USA and other countries to promote a political solution and support a government of national reconciliation there.

Afghanistan urgently needed help to heal the wounds of the war and the division of society. This could only happen if all the leading powers adopted a common position. Unfortunately, our negotiating partners – the USA and Pakistan above all – did not want to take this path with us.

They had other plans. For them, Afghanistan was part of a giant chessboard on which they wanted to play with various figures, including bandits and terrorists.

We all know the outcome of this game. In the 1990s, Afghanistan was probably the main breeding ground for the terrorist threat. It was no coincidence that Al-Qaeda leader Osama bin Laden chose it as a safe haven. And on 11 September 2001, we all watched the terrible attacks on the World Trade Center live on television.

Part II

Understanding the Global World

Who Benefits from Globalization?

We cannot understand any of the central problems of our modern world unless we look at them in the context of global processes. 'We live in a global world' – this phrase has been circulating for several decades now. At the start of this book, I wrote that we have not yet understood the globalized world. This lack of understanding – in terms of politics, economics and the environment – is becoming increasingly dangerous.

The end of the Cold War gave a powerful impetus to globalization. Once we had accomplished this, through joint efforts, we developed plans for a new world order in the hopes of solving many global problems.

Unfortunately, these processes have worked out differently from how we imagined things at the time. Globalization turned into a spontaneous process, intensifying many existing contradictions and conflicts. At the same time, it increased imbalances between the various regions of the world.

The leading industrialized countries and their multinational corporations used globalization processes to further their own interests. Big developing countries like China and India were able to successfully adapt to global processes, but in many other developing countries there are more losers than winners. For this reason, many people consider globalization to be a new version of colonialism.

Even in the most developed countries, far from everyone has benefited from globalization in its current form. This is why we are experiencing a wave of populism in numerous countries and the rise of parties and politicians who can amass the votes of the dissatisfied. In many cases, people are being beguiled by veritable demagogues. But the dissatisfaction of millions of citizens is real and there are serious reasons for it.

The hope that globalization as we know it would lead to faster development and the resolution of problems within countries and on a global level has not been fulfilled. For example, there has been no real progress in resolving the global problem of poverty. Although China and India, above all, have managed to lift many millions of citizens out of poverty, it remains a bitter reality for hundreds of millions of others around the world.

Understanding the global world is a task of enormous complexity, as is finding solutions to the challenges it poses.

After the end of the Cold War, economists and business-people proclaimed the worldwide victory of capitalism. To put it more precisely, they celebrated the triumph of a certain economic model: the neoliberal 'free market' in which the state relinquishes many of the obligations it has towards its citizens. The model of the social market economy, which enabled Europe to rise from the ashes after the horrors of the First World War, was – so it was said – a thing of the past. The new global economy was to be based on the standard model of the so-called 'Washington Consensus', summarized as competition, deregulation and privatization.

Nearly thirty years have passed since then, and it is high time to take stock. The verdict may still be preliminary, but it is also more than sobering. At the 2019 meeting of the World Economic Forum in Davos, even the assembled politicians and captains of industry had to admit as much. The problem of global inequality was at the heart of their debates.

We should give credit to the organizers of the forum for commissioning Oxfam, an NGO known for its studies of the problems of poverty, underdevelopment and inequality, to compile a report on this issue. Its findings were publicized around the world. Since the financial crisis of 2007–8, the number of dollar billionaires has doubled worldwide to more than two thousand. In 2018 alone, the billionaires' income rose by $900 billion – an increase of two and a half billion per day; the total wealth of the twenty-six richest people in the world – $1.4 trillion – corresponded to the income of 3.8 billion of the world's poorest inhabitants. Today, nearly 750 million people live in poverty and have an income of less than $5.5 per day.

It is apparent that the people who control the most capital are also the ones best adapted to globalization and getting the most benefit from it. The finance structures associated with them keep producing bubbles and literally create money from nothing. Put simply, their principle is the privatization of profit and socialization of loss.

This is not just a question of unequal incomes, but also of unequal opportunities – first and foremost, in people's access to medical care and education. This is why the life expectancy of the poor is twenty years shorter on average than that of the rich. And since they are unable to receive a quality education, it is not easy for them to escape poverty. A vicious cycle.

The standard of living of the middle class – the foundation of the economy and democracy – has also stagnated in the past decades. US researchers are worried about this. Since 1979, the real income of Americans who are generally considered to be middle class has grown by only 28 per cent; the real income of the richest people has grown by 95 per cent in the same period.

How can all of this happen in an age of tremendous advances in science, technology and economics? The main reason is a tax system that seems to be tailored to the interests of the rich, and particularly to the richest of all. Tax rates in the upper brackets go down year after year, and the rich regularly receive new tax benefits and incentives from the state – not to mention the fact that globalization offers them new ways of hiding their money from the tax authorities and protecting it in offshore havens.

Here is a striking figure: in the USA, on average, just four cents per dollar of the state's tax revenue comes from the rich. The rest is paid by ordinary citizens, including the poor. In the UK, the poorest 10 per cent of the population spends a higher proportion of its income on taxes than does the richest 10 per cent.

Of course, tax policy lies entirely in the hands of each country and cannot be changed by 'directives' that are binding for all states. But what we are dealing with here is a global trend that has grown stronger in the past decades. One way or another, we have not yet escaped the temptations of the ideology of 'a free market and small government' that has spread throughout the world since the days of Ronald Reagan and Margaret Thatcher. I think the time has come for politicians who would reverse this development.

Furthermore, inequality and social injustice are increasingly hindering the economy and slowing economic growth. Many economists, and even billionaires such as Warren Buffet, Mark Zuckerberg and Steven Rockefeller, are writing and talking about this.

Ultimately, it is necessary to overhaul the globally dominant economic model of a largely unbridled market economy with its goal of maximum profit and maximum consumption. This system produces crises, social inequality and the danger of an environmental catastrophe.

The new model, which we must adopt in an evolutionary way but quite rapidly, should be founded on a combination of market-based and private initiatives, the principles of corporate social and environmental responsibility, and effective state regulation.

We must rethink the aims of economic activity. Consumption cannot be the main and nearly sole impulse for growth. New standards are required for the economy

– namely, public goods such as a sustainable environment, a healthy population in the broadest sense, education, culture and social cohesion, including bridging the gap between prosperity and poverty.

The Evolution of the State

It will be impossible to solve the above-mentioned problems unless the state takes on a prominent role – and not just individual states, but also intergovernmental and international organizations. We cannot simply hope that the free market and free trade will fix everything. It is time for even the most fervent supporters of this economic system to look reality in the eye and stop denigrating the role of the state.

The debate about the right relationship between the public and private sectors will probably never end. I have always tried to stand on the side of common sense in this debate. I believe it is wrong to equate the state with the bureaucratic machine. Bureaucracy may well deserve criticism, but criticizing bureaucracy should not degenerate into a wholesale negation of state governance. We in Russia remember the price we had to pay for this in the 1990s. The collapse of the state deprived millions of people of their jobs, their savings and their life prospects, and it led to flourishing organized crime, corruption and the seizure of real power by oligarchs.

For historical reasons, different countries have different ratios of public and private ownership and different degrees of state regulation. This is the problem with the 'recommendations' or demands of organizations such as the International Monetary Fund, which try to lump all countries together. Experience has shown that countries that reject such advice and instead shape their own economic policy, like China and Malaysia, only benefit from doing so. The decisive factor is that the state must be responsible and accountable to its citizens. In the end, only a state like this will gain the trust of its people.

Development Goals

At the Millennium Summit in September 2000, eight concrete goals for socioeconomic development were set by 189 UN member states: to eradicate poverty and hunger; to guarantee universal primary education; to make progress in the direction of true gender equality; to reduce child mortality; to improve maternal health; to combat AIDS, malaria and other diseases; to ensure environmental sustainability; to develop a global partnership for development.

These Millennium Development Goals, enshrined in a document signed at the highest level, defined the responsibilities of governments and the role of partnerships between industrialized and developing countries. The decision was made to review the implementation of the goals in 2015.

Time passed, and many observers – myself included – repeatedly complained that the UN member states were not doing enough to reach the agreed targets. Many industrialized countries withdrew from the partnership, huge sums of money were still being spent on defence, and not all the developing countries acted fully in accordance with the goals.

Nonetheless, it is clear that this UN project achieved important results. The number of people living in extreme poverty has more than halved in the past two decades, as has the proportion of undernourished people in developing countries. We have almost reached the goal of universal primary education: today, more than 90 per cent of children in developing countries attend school. Successes have been achieved in the fight against AIDS, malaria and tuberculosis. Child and maternal mortality and the number of people without access to clean drinking water have decreased by half.

There is still a lot to do. Progress has not been made to the same degree everywhere. Hundreds of millions of people are still suffering from poverty, disease and discrimination. But there is no denying that the joint efforts of states, international organizations, civil society, science and business have produced results. Together we can aim high and accomplish the most difficult tasks.

The Environmental Challenge

The great challenges and problems of the modern world are all closely intertwined. As I see it, there are two central threats, both of which could undo all our attempts to ensure a decent life for present and future generations. First, there is the danger of a new and devastating war involving the use of weapons of mass destruction. Second, there is the threat of environmental catastrophe as a result of accelerated global warming, which is undeniably in large part a manmade problem.

Over the years, the protection of our environment has become a personal and daily concern for me. In 1993, I was involved in the founding of Green Cross International, an environmental organization that brings together dedicated people in dozens of countries. But I had started to worry even before this, when I saw with my own eyes how nature can punish people for their irresponsible behaviour.

This worry is now shared by hundreds of millions of people on all continents. The impressive success of the Greens in the European Parliament elections in May 2019 is indicative of this. In the spring of the same year, tens of thousands of young people around the world took to the streets with a clear message: we must take measures now to save our planet from a climate catastrophe. These young people understand what many older people apparently cannot grasp – namely, that we are dealing with the very survival of humanity. The window of opportunity is closing, and delaying the fight against climate change is almost as dangerous as being in total denial about the problem.

Global environmental threats are the flip side, the inevitable consequence of the existing economic model and the industrial and technical-economic solutions associated with it. These threats cannot be eliminated in a national context alone, and often not even through existing forms of international cooperation. Global risks are, above all, the expression of a new form of global interdependence. They therefore call for new forms of international cooperation.

According to the Global Risks Report, which is compiled each year by experts from the World Economic Forum in Davos, climate change, the lack of a coordinated effort between states to protect the environment and the lack of investment in infrastructures for disaster prevention are all among the top ten or even top five risks facing humanity over the next decade. Extreme weather events (storms, floods) and a failure to adapt to climate change and natural disasters (earthquakes, tsunamis, volcanic eruptions) are the top-ranking threats forecast for the near future.

We pump, process, consume and waste huge amounts of our planet's resources.

In the coming years, humanity will run a serious risk of depleting the resources needed to support the growing global population. While 700 million people around the world are starving today, around one third of all food – 1.3 billion tonnes per year – is not reaching consumers but is instead rotting away and winding up in landfills and waste incinerators.

In the report produced by the International Assessment of Agricultural Knowledge, Science and Technology for Development (IAASTD) Project, 400 experts from UN member states issued a warning: our current methods of industrial agricultural production and our use of resources are undermining the regulation mechanisms created by nature.

Forecasts show that the demand for food and animal feed will grow by 70 per cent in the coming decades, but 60 per cent of the world's most important ecosystems on which these resources depend have already been damaged or are being plundered. Since 1970, humanity has wiped out 60 per cent of all mammals, birds, fish and reptiles. This prompted the world's leading experts to warn that the extinction of wildlife has led to an emergency situation that threatens our very civilization.

The IAASTD report tells us that the extinction rate for various animal and plant species is unprecedented in the history of the planet. It is dozens or hundreds of times higher than the average rates over the past 10 million years. A million of the species found on Earth are now threatened. Scientists are talking about the danger of the 'destruction of nature'. They warn that humans are undermining the Earth's ability to generate drinking water, clean air and productive soil.

As a result of our economic activities, half of the tropical rainforests – the lungs of our ecosystems – have already disappeared. At the current rate of exploitation, only 10 per cent will remain by the year 2030. We are poisoning seas and rivers at an unimaginable pace. Every day, 2 million tons of sewage, as well as industrial and agricultural waste, flow into the world's water reservoir; 80 per cent of rivers around the world are currently in danger.

According to the World Water Development Report published in 2019, one out of every three of the planet's inhabitants has no access to clean drinking water, and six out of ten have no access to clean sanitary and hygienic facilities.

Air pollution and contaminated water kill more people every year than all wars and acts of violence put together. More than smoking, hunger or natural disasters. More than AIDS, tuberculosis and malaria. A study published in 2017 in the medical journal *The Lancet* revealed that, each year, more than nine million people worldwide die of diseases associated with the toxic effects of environmental pollution. The annual losses due to premature deaths amount to around $4.6 trillion per year, which corresponds to 6.2 per cent of the global economy.

Global Warming

The World Meteorological Association has sounded the alarm: the global warming process is speeding up, and the growing concentration of greenhouse gases is causing global temperatures to rise to an ever more dangerous level. Scientists have reported a record rise in sea levels and high temperatures on land and at sea since the early 2010s. This warming trend has been apparent since the start of the century and is likely to continue.

Based on the latest data, the concentration of carbon dioxide in the atmosphere since the mid-twentieth century is 150 per cent higher than in the pre-industrial age. There was a similar concentration of greenhouse gases around 3–5 million years ago, when the temperature was two to three degrees higher than now and the average sea level was ten to fifteen metres higher than it is today.

There is no doubt that the temperature rise combined with population growth will greatly increase the probability of conflicts and will endanger our security and stability. The world economy will take a severe blow. Scientists at Stanford University have calculated that the global GDP will fall by 15 per cent even if the nations of the world stick to the framework of the Paris climate agreement (which seems unlikely) and the air temperature rises by up to 2.5 degrees. If the temperature rises by 3°C, the global GDP will fall by 25 per cent. If nothing is done and the temperature climbs by 4°C by the year 2100, the global GDP will decrease by more than 30 per cent compared to 2010.

Life itself refutes the claim that efforts to save our planet from a climate catastrophe will supposedly hurt the economy.

We still have a decade in which to make a change. This is the conclusion reached by scientists from the Intergovernmental Panel on Climate Change (IPCC). To avoid the most devastating effects of climate change, the world must lower its carbon dioxide emissions by 45 per cent by the year 2030 and completely abandon the use of hydrocarbons by 2050.

This goal is truly ambitious. In order to reach it, revolutionary changes are needed in the use of natural resources, and fundamental changes are required in the areas of energy, industry, agriculture, fishing and transportation as well as in the behaviour of producers and consumers. But there is no other way. The existing model is unsustainable. It continually generates crises, social inequality and a growing danger of environmental disaster.

To be fair, I must say that there have been some encouraging trends. The European Union supported the recommendation to refuse any new trade deals with countries that have not signed the Paris Agreement. France will close all of its coal-fired power plants by 2021. India recently abandoned its plans to build such plants. China has banned 500 car models with inefficient fuel consumption.

New technologies and technical solutions already make it possible to supply energy at lower prices than fossil fuels. In economically leading countries, solar and wind power are becoming the cheapest sources of energy.

To date, 55 countries, 140 of the largest companies and hundreds of cities have committed themselves to switching entirely to renewable energy.

According to experts, the global economy will make a profit of $26 trillion by 2030 if nations and large companies invest more in clean energy. A rise in investment volume could create around 65 million new jobs by 2030.

We are not helpless in the fight against a climate

catastrophe. We have ideas, we have solutions, we have technical and financial possibilities. Adopting a new form of environmental and political thinking, as difficult as it may be, can lead us to a world that is much more stable, secure, successful and fair than the world in which we currently live.

The Earth Charter

Overcoming the environmental challenge depends above all on changing the attitudes of politicians, businesspeople and ordinary citizens. This was the goal of Green Cross International and the Earth Council initiative led by Maurice Strong, a well-known Canadian political and public figure. In 1994, we launched a comprehensive international consultation process for developing the Earth Charter.

The international commission spent three years formulating the fundamental principles of this document. Subsequently, more than 100,000 people in fifty-one countries around the world were involved in its creation.

The basic idea behind the Earth Charter can be summed up in a single sentence: 'To save humanity and all future generations of people, we must save the Earth.'

The sixteen basic principles of the charter relate to environmental protection, individual rights, eradicating poverty, affirming gender equality and promoting a culture of peace. As you can see, we went beyond purely environmental issues in the Earth Charter, but we had good reasons for doing so. The project participants unanimously agreed that these principles were all connected.

I would like to list them here in full:

I   Respect and Care for the Community of Life
    1   Respect Earth and life in all its diversity.
    2   Care for the community of life with understanding, compassion and love.

3 Build democratic societies that are just, participatory, sustainable and peaceful.

4 Secure Earth's bounty and beauty for present and future generations.

II Ecological Integrity

5 Protect and restore the integrity of Earth's ecological systems, with special concern for biological diversity and the natural processes that sustain life.

6 Prevent harm as the best method of environmental protection and, when knowledge is limited, apply a precautionary approach.

7 Adopt patterns of production, consumption and reproduction that safeguard Earth's regenerative capacities, human rights and community well-being.

8 Advance the study of ecological sustainability and promote the open exchange and wide application of the knowledge acquired.

III Social and Economic Justice

9 Eradicate poverty as an ethical, social and environmental imperative.

10 Ensure that economic activities and institutions at all levels promote human development in an equitable and sustainable manner.

11 Affirm gender equality and equity as prerequisites to sustainable development and ensure universal access to education, health care and economic opportunity.

12 Uphold the right of all, without discrimination, to a natural and social environment supportive of human dignity, bodily health and spiritual well-being, with special attention to the rights of indigenous peoples and minorities.

IV Democracy, Nonviolence and Peace

13 Strengthen democratic institutions at all levels,

  and provide transparency and accountability in governance, inclusive participation in decision-making and access to justice.

14 Integrate into formal education and lifelong learning the knowledge, values and skills needed for a sustainable way of life.

15 Treat all living beings with respect and consideration.

16 Promote a culture of tolerance, nonviolence and peace.

This document, which outlines the fundamental principles for environmentally sustainable development, and is also a wonderful primer for a new ethics, was first published in Paris on 12 March 2000.

We naturally wondered at the time how this manifesto, which we had put our hearts into, would be received. We soon found out: the Earth Charter reached people and began to have an effect. It was officially supported by thousands of organizations, including UNESCO, the World Conservation Union, the United States Conference of Mayors, national and international university associations and hundreds of cities in dozens of countries.

UNESCO adopted a resolution to 'recognize the Earth Charter as an important ethical framework for sustainable development, and acknowledge its ethical principles, its objectives and its contents'. It recommends using the Earth Charter as an educational tool.

In the Russian Republic of Tatarstan, the ideas of the Earth Charter were supported by all branches of government. Tatarstan was the first region in the world to put the Earth Charter to practical use.

Our document is aimed first and foremost at civil society. I am proud to have contributed to its formulation. Our thanks go to Princess Beatrix of the Netherlands and former Prime Minister of the Netherlands Ruud Lubbers for their political support, as well as to Maurice Strong, Steven Rockefeller – who led the drafting committee – and all the committee members.

I believe that the charter specifies ethical and moral guidelines that are urgently needed by humanity in the new millennium.

New Threats

Ethical guidelines are increasingly important in science. I have always held science and scientists in high regard. The speed with which scientific discoveries were made in the twentieth century was unprecedented. I was especially impressed by one figure in particular: over 90 per cent of our scientific information in the fields of physics, chemistry and biology, and our scientific ideas about the structure of the world, are the result of research conducted in the last century and a half. Implemented in the form of modern technologies, science has massively changed people's lives.

But the twentieth century also experienced the dark side of scientific and technological progress. One classic example of this is the work of German scientist Fritz Haber, who received the Nobel Prize for Chemistry in 1918. His research resulted in the production of chemical fertilizers – and the invention of chemical weapons that plague humanity to this day.

With the advent of the nuclear missile age, the problem intensified and the threat grew to become a key question of human survival. The rapid scientific and technological advances of this age were placed at the service of the military-industrial complex. The economy and business became heavily dependent on military contracts. Of course, some scientific and technological achievements made their way from the military into civilian life, but this kind of 'drug dependency' not only leads to the diversion of massive sums of money, it also harbours a deadly risk.

Although the nuclear arms race was stopped in the 1980s and 1990s, the dangers associated with the military use of the latest technologies still remain.

Military technological rivalry is now breaking out of its restrictive boundaries and extending into new areas. The evolution of science and technology creates new threats for our planet and for humanity. Yes, knowledge is power, but it is also risky. In a global, fast-changing world, scientific breakthroughs can be dangerous unless the world community learns how to assess and control this risk.

The technologies of the twenty-first century include artificial intelligence, robotics, nanotechnology, genetic engineering, cloning, experiments with virtual reality and other promising fields. Like most people, I do not know exactly what is taking place in each of these areas, but we can be certain that a lot of surprising and unforeseen things will happen. I see a danger in allowing the knowledge and use of new technologies to lie in the hands of relatively small groups of people. What guarantee do we have that these people will always act with forethought and in a morally correct way?

In 2018, a news item circulated around the world: at an international conference, a Chinese scientist announced the birth of the first genetically manipulated babies. Their genome had apparently been modified so the children would have an inborn immunity to AIDS. This raises the prospect of deliberate 'genetic programming', 'designer babies' and similar marvels.

The main question here is whether it is time to allow humans to interfere with the genetic code of our own species? After all, even the consequences of the wide-scale use of genetically modified plants have not yet been fully clarified. The demand for controls on research in the field of genetic engineering springs not from a vague fear of the future but from a sensible precautionary approach.

The risks associated with new research in the fields of artificial intelligence and robotics are probably just as great. Several decades ago, the American science fiction writer Isaac Asimov posed the problem of the relationship between humans and the robots created by them. His warnings are perhaps even more pertinent now than they were back when he wrote his novels.

The main principle should be responsibility. Humanity must not allow such complex and potentially dangerous processes to slip from its grasp. Society as a whole should be involved in decisions about the use of scientific discoveries. Questions associated with the application of new technologies are socioeconomic and, ultimately, political in nature.

We currently face the question of which mechanisms must be installed on a national and international level to ensure that the limitless possibilities of the human intellect do not endanger the future of humanity. I believe that, out of concern for future generations, we must exercise reasonable caution.

Yet Another Stern Reminder

In 2020, a new calamity has been inflicted upon humankind and has ushered in a new global challenge. The coronavirus epidemic has engulfed the whole world in the space of two or three months. If at first there seemed to be hope that it would prove containable, scientists were soon issuing warnings to the contrary. These warnings, unfortunately, went unheeded by a host of leaders and politicians. The epidemic then proceeded to sweep all before it, developing into a pandemic and necessitating unprecedented measures and decisions. And so we have found ourselves in a new reality.

This crisis provides us with yet further confirmation of the fragility of the global world – a world fraught with the danger of sliding into chaos.

It has already become commonplace to argue that, once we prevail over this invisible enemy and put this calamity behind us, the world will not be what it was before the outbreak. But what exactly *will* it be like? That depends on what lessons we learn from the events currently unfolding before our eyes.

I return, in this connection, to the history of our struggle against the nuclear peril. We realized that this was our common enemy, our common threat, whereupon the leaders of two countries, the USSR and the USA, declared that a nuclear war cannot be won and must never be fought. What followed was Reykjavík and the first treaties eliminating nuclear weapons. And yet, even with 85 per cent of those nuclear arsenals now destroyed, the threat remains, and will not disappear completely until humanity does away with all weapons of mass destruction.

Other global threats remain, of course, and are actually intensifying: poverty and inequality, water scarcity, environmental degradation and global warming, the depletion of oceanic and terrestrial resources, the migration crisis. And now we have a new reminder of yet another formidable challenge – diseases and epidemics capable of ravaging a global, interconnected world with unprecedented speed.

This all-sweeping calamity serves to remind us all that, when it comes to certain threats, we cannot simply 'hunker down', or 'sit things out', or 'turn a blind eye': there's no hiding from them – not any more! Furthermore, the response to this new challenge cannot be purely 'national' in character. Yes, national governments now shoulder immense responsibilities and find themselves compelled to make the most difficult of decisions. But, much like other global problems, the problem we are currently facing cannot in principle be solved exclusively at the national level.

The main thing we need to grasp – of this I am convinced – is that our understanding of *security* must now change. Historically, and even after the end of the Cold War, the tendency has been to reduce this notion primarily to its military dimension, and in recent years, we've heard nothing but talk of armaments, missiles, airstrikes …

In the first few months of 2020, the world has already been on the brink of clashes involving great powers, with serious hostilities in Iran, in Iraq, in Syria. And though the participants eventually stepped back, it was the same dangerous and reckless policy of brinkmanship.

Is it not clear that wars and arms races do not solve the global problems of today? War is the defeat – the failure of politics!

Together with my friends in the Forum of Nobel Peace Laureates, we have for years been calling for a radical rethinking of international politics. Let me quote from our appeal adopted back in 2005: 'Focusing on meeting human needs and having a reverence for life are the foundation of human security. Excessive military expenditure actually breeds insecurity. Two areas where funds need to be channelled by the international community are education and health, particularly regarding the scourges of AIDS, malaria and tuberculosis through both protection and prevention.' What could one add to this? Just the name of the new dreadful disease.

It is human security that must be our utmost priority today. This means providing people with food and water; it means protecting the environment; it means giving absolute precedence to human health. To safeguard human security, we must develop strategies, make plans and preparations, create reserves. And the responsibility for doing so must lie with heads of state and government as well as leaders at all levels.

But even this won't be enough if governments continue

to fling immense sums into the furnace of a new arms race. Today, it is overwhelmingly clear that resources must be redirected from military ventures and into human security projects.

And so I'll never tire of repeating: we need to demilitarize global politics, international relations and political thinking. To address this at the highest international level, I called, in early April, for an emergency session of the United Nations General Assembly to be convened as soon as the situation stabilizes. It should be about nothing less than revising the entire global agenda. Specifically, I propose that all states commit to reducing their military budgets by at least 10–15 per cent. This is the least they should do now, as a first step towards a new consciousness, a new civilization.

The section 'Yet Another Stern Reminder'
translated by Leo Shtutin

Part III

Ideas and Politics

The Wave of Populism and Decline of Democracy

The world of the twenty-first century has been inundated with problems. We have to admit that we were poorly prepared to solve them. By 'we', I mean world leaders and political parties, as well as society as a whole. But people want to see action being taken, and they have a tool for asserting this demand and calling on politicians to find answers to unresolved questions. This tool – practically the only one they possess – is their ability to vote in elections.

Demonstrations, street protests, strikes – all of these are legitimate within the framework of the law, but voters are the ones who have the final say. And for the past couple of decades, they have increasingly voted differently than expected by the traditional political parties, which have passed governance back and forth between them for many decades. Today, more and more politicians and parties generally described as 'populist' are coming to power.

The parties that represented the political spectrum in the epoch now past looked to ideologies with roots in the nineteenth century. The most important of these were liberalism, conservatism and social democracy. Today, it has emerged that none of these ideologies, either individually or collectively, has answers to the challenges of the new millennium. Are we therefore experiencing the decline, or even the end, of these ideologies?

Before attempting to answer this question, I want to return to the topic of populism. Who votes for populists? The vast majority are ordinary people who worry about the future of their country, their families and their children. They are the globalization losers who formerly identified as middle class but who now find their standard of living in constant decline.

Statistics show that, over the past decades, the real income of the middle class in most industrialized countries has not risen but has actually decreased. This is despite tremendous scientific advances, new technologies and the digitization of all aspects of life. One might think that all these achievements would open up undreamed-of prospects for human civilization and every single individual. This has not been the case.

Is it any wonder, then, that voters are turning against traditional parties and opting instead for those people who mercilessly criticize such parties and swear to 'put the house in order' and 'drain the swamp'? These are mostly empty and entirely unfounded promises. Moreover, they do not improve the life circumstances of those who, as a result of the upheavals of recent decades, have wound up on the losing side. On the contrary, they just make the rich even richer.

I cannot simply condemn those who vote for political demagogues, however. It has always been human nature to hope and to look for political heroes. Furthermore, people apparently see no other way of signalling to the political system and its representatives that something has to change.

This is what goes through my mind when I watch television and see the faces of those who have given their vote to populists and demagogues. They are not to blame. Whether the representatives they elect will find solutions to the current problems and challenges is another matter. I suspect there will be bitter disappointments. In politics, there are no easy answers – and no panaceas.

We Need New Ideas

All political movements today are searching for new concepts, innovations, viable ideas. Yet I would warn against prematurely declaring the death of the ideologies inherited from the past. They are powerful intellectual currents whose potential is nowhere near exhausted.

In their modern form, Christian democracy and social democracy, conservatism and liberalism have much in common. In particular, they all rely on the values of democracy, human rights and the rule of law. But they propose different solutions to the concrete problems affecting our society. How can the security of the people and the state be guaranteed? What must be done for people to be able to live in a healthy environment? How can poverty, social divides and inequality be overcome? How can the problem of migration and cultural differences be solved, and how can peace and understanding be established between religions?

No one knows the definitive answers to all these questions. There aren't any. The world is changing all the time, and a solution that satisfies the majority today may be considered inadequate or outdated tomorrow.

I have lived a long life, participated in the battle of ideas and measured these ideas against reality. In doing so, I have come to the conclusion that different ideological and political movements have enriched the human spirit and contributed to human progress each in their own way.

I was always willing to engage in dialogue with representatives of the conservative camp or dedicated proponents of a free market. But I make no secret of the fact that the ideas of social democracy have always been closest to my heart. I still believe they hold promise, and I am convinced that they can help lay the conceptual foundation for a future social order. Of course, other ideological and political movements will also play their part in this; each will bring its own convictions and principles to the table. For me, however, social democratic thought has been a guiding light for many years.

Social Democracy Yesterday and Today

Social democracy arose on the left wing of the political spectrum and split into various directions in the twentieth century. In Russia, the Bolsheviks cut off all lines of development with the exception of their own extreme communist one. The path they chose involved the nationalization of the economy, an ideological monopoly and a one-party system. This led to the emergence of a totalitarian state that was far removed from the ideals of freedom and democracy.

We ourselves came to realize that we had to abandon this path. Yet we must not forget that millions of people in our country believed in socialism and its ideals, and they also believed in a just society. I believed in this, too – and I continue to believe in it, now in its contemporary, social-democratic interpretation.

I joined the Communist Party of the Soviet Union in 1950 after consulting with my father and grandfather. My grandfather was a veteran communist, and my father joined the party on the front line during the war. I would never deny the sincere convictions and selfless work of these generations. But life changes all the time, and it brought us to the realization that Russia needs a social-democratic project. Indeed, the whole world needs social democracy. Without it, the political and democratic process would be incomplete.

However, the conditions for social democracy and the forces of the left appear unfavourable in Europe and the rest of the world today. The 'shift to the right' continues. The radical right and nationalist parties are growing stronger, while social democrats in a number of countries are losing votes.

The surge in right-wing nationalist forces is looking more and more like a pan-European or even transatlantic movement, with its own ideologists, massive financial support and backing among the mass media.

Left-wing parties have been particularly hard hit by the disappointment of many voters in the political establishment, while traditional right-wing parties are finding themselves forced to join coalitions with the extreme right.

While this tendency has recently intensified, it is not new, and its causes were apparent early on. Back in September 1992, at the Congress of the Socialist International, I said: 'The weakening of the left that is seen nearly everywhere today is not in the interest of democracy. The strengthening of right-wing radical, nationalist and fundamentalist tendencies should be a warning to us regarding the forces that could fill the political vacuum left behind if the forces of the left retreat.'

The consequence of all this could be a new form of authoritarianism in a more or less 'soft' version that would operate on a global scale. European social democracy under-estimated this development for a long time and has yet to find a convincing response to it.

Moving Forward in a Changing World

One should speak openly to friends and like-minded individuals, and I must say that, in the past decades, social democrats allowed themselves to swim in the waves of monetarism, economic liberalism and globalization without fundamentally questioning them. At most, they tried to mitigate the worst effects. Left-wing forces prioritized the discussion of problems such as the position of women, minorities, migrants and other largely sociocultural issues. These are important topics, of course, but a great deal was overlooked, particularly the problems and concerns of workers, the middle class – the ordinary people who were losing their jobs and sometimes even their livelihood.

Furthermore, non-socialist European parties such as the Christian Democratic Union (CDU) in Germany integrated social-democratic values such as solidarity, equality (of opportunities) and social justice in their agenda. It is an open question as to whether, under these conditions, social democracy had the room for ideological and political manoeuvre. In any case, the pendulum swung to the right.

At the moment, however, it seems to be moving the other way again. It comes as a surprise to a number of people that signs of this can be seen in the United States. For the first time in many years, multiple candidates in the run-up to the elections have been adopting positions of democratic socialism. A lively debate is under way about a national health care system based on socialist values, and a 'Green New Deal', which brings together the goals of the environmental movement and the active role of the state, in the spirit of Roosevelt's New Deal.

In France, the nationalist forces around Marine Le Pen were defeated in the second round of presidential elections. In Spain, a coalition led by Pedro Sánchez of the Socialist Workers' Party came to power. And in the UK, the Labour Party has shifted significantly to the left.

Do the left, socialists and social democrats just need to wait until the pendulum of history puts them back in power? No: waiting would be a serious mistake.

Now more than ever it is necessary to seek a new intellectual and political basis for the left-wing movement. Societies everywhere are changing quickly and irrevocably. Social democracy has to change, too, if it is to move forward. However, left-wing and social-democratic values must not be watered down, much less sacrificed in the process. The ordinary citizens for whom social democracy has to fight – the workers, the middle class, the majority of the population – must not be let down. This should not be a fight for their votes alone, it should be a fight for them to lead a decent life.

Can Politics and Morals
Be Reconciled?

Social democrats must take a leading role in solving a major issue in humanity's current phase of development: reconciling politics and morals. This task is exceptionally difficult but it cannot be delayed.

We have seen countless examples of immorality and corruption in politics in recent years. Politicians all over the world, even heads of state and government, have placed themselves above the most basic ethical norms. How could it have come to this? The answer is not to be found in the courts that have convicted politicians and officials for such transgressions. Instead, this is a job for society.

Something is not right in the political culture and the mindset of the political class. Cynicism, fighting for votes at any cost and luring voters with promises as pretty as they are impossible to keep have practically become the rule. It is a short path from here to corruption and criminal behaviour.

The more this spreads, the more deeply people will come to believe that politics is, in essence, a dirty and immoral business. I emphatically reject this idea.

In the perestroika years, we made it our goal to bridge the gap between politics and morals. This idea was not new, but we sought to put it into practice on the level of the party and the state. Our most important tool for doing so was glasnost.

Today, not just our country but the whole world needs glasnost: transparent governance, true accountability to the people on the part of the powerful, freedom and a sense of responsibility in the mass media. Voters will place their trust in politicians who present serious, realistic programmes and in those who point out effective mechanisms for guaranteeing honesty and incorruptibility on the part of the government.

The moral aspect is just as important in foreign policy. Here, too, we have seen many examples of cynicism and immorality in the past decades. Whole countries have been subjected to immoral experiments, be it for the sake of 'promoting democracy', under the pretence that they possessed weapons of mass destruction, or because supposedly oppressed national minorities were in need of protection. The fact that such problems (assuming they really existed) can be solved using peaceful political means was ignored. International law was ignored, as was morality.

To justify the most egregious violations of international law, it is often argued that there are contradictions in this law, such as between the right to self-determination and respect for the territorial integrity of states. I see no contradiction here, as long as the process of self-determination takes place within a constitutional framework. Above all, however, we must never forget the key principle of international law: the peaceful settlement of disputes. This must be the basis for the existence of our modern world.

Morals, ethics and certain rules of conduct must be firmly anchored in world politics. There has been much talk in the West recently about a 'rules-based international order', but no one has explained exactly what this means – and, at the same time, Russia is accused of violating this order.

I agree that we need rules. One of them must be that we take not only our own interests into account, but also the interests of other countries – and not just in bilateral relations. To return to an example mentioned earlier, when NATO and the EU expanded, the Western partners assured Russia that it had no reason to worry and it would not be affected. Russia was presented with a *fait accompli*. But it is obvious that these decisions did affect the security of our country because they involved our neighbours, with whom we share a centuries-old history.

International relations must not be based on the rule of force or solely pragmatic considerations that take no account of historical, cultural factors or – I will say it again – morality. This is one of the most important lessons of the past decades.

The Articles of Faith of the New Thinking

The path we took in the years that ended the Cold War and the following decades was not easy. There were many dramatic events, and there were both successes and disappointments. But before turning to my vision for how this path might continue, and what role might be played by states, international organizations and civil society in the coming years, I would like to set out a kind of credo of new political thinking. I want to recount the principles and guiding ideas that we adopted back then and that, I believe, remain valid to this day.

- Human civilization has reached a point at which interconnection and interdependence between all of its parts call for a new kind of world politics. Politics based on confrontation – between states and ideologies – must become a thing of the past.
- The nuclear age poses a danger to the existence of humanity. Humanity has grown fragile and is at risk of being destroyed. This danger cannot be overcome without ultimately eliminating nuclear weapons. There can be no other goal.
- Differences between states must be resolved only through peaceful means, with the help of dialogue and negotiation.

If we continue to use the old methods for resolving international conflicts – war, conquest, subjugation and gaining an advantage at the expense of others – it will lead to mortal danger for everyone.

- The only arbitrator with the right to permit the use of military force in exceptional cases in order to counter aggression is the United Nations. Military actions by states that view themselves as the world police are unacceptable.

- The tightly intertwined global economy makes all states dependent on one another. Regional and global integration is a difficult, contradictory process, but it is unavoidable and should benefit all countries.

- Relations between states old and new, large and small, must be based on a balance of interests. This balance can be achieved if everyone involved brings good will to the table.

- The differences between states, the aspects that make them unique, are no cause for dispute and enmity. On the contrary, they are what make cooperation, the exchange of experiences and values, and progress possible.

- Morals, universal values, respect for the individual, for human dignity – all of this must become an integral component of world politics and international relations.

- Democratization of society and democratization of international relations are two facets of a global trend. Each country should be free to choose which path it wants to take. No one may force their own interpretation of democracy on another, especially not through the use of arms.

- Armed forces should be developed on the basis of reasonable sufficiency for defence. An arms race is wasteful and immoral; it harms the economy and leads to hostility and confrontation.

- Ensuring peace is the most important prerequisite for

overcoming global problems such as the environmental crisis, international terrorism, migration and all the other challenges on which states and international organizations must focus.

- In this new epoch of ours, civil society and its organizations are becoming increasingly important players in international relations. Political leaders have an obligation and special responsibility to look to civil society and include it in the process of solving problems of security and development.

Some will find these principles completely self-evident or even banal. I see it differently. If this were the case, it would be easy to implement these principles in international relations. But think of how difficult it has been to take every single step based on them. And think of how often they have been violated recently.

I firmly believe that these principles offer the prospect of a better world. They are what we should be striving for. No single country can set the course for achieving this ideal. This raises the question of leadership, one of the most urgent and difficult challenges in world politics today.

Part IV

Who's Who in the Global World?

The USA: Monopoly Leadership or Partnership?

After the end of the Cold War, the United States basked in a sense of triumph and claimed a monopoly on leadership in world politics. Moreover, politicians, experts and journalists began speaking of a new American empire. As a consequence, both the atmosphere and, above all, the rhetoric changed. The role of the USA on the world stage changed as well – and not for the better.

The United States was our most important partner in ending the Cold War and the arms race. We always accorded a special importance to our relations with this country, because we were aware of its economic strength, its military power and its political influence. Without a shift in our relationship with America and our dialogue with Washington, there would have been no decisive changes in the world at the end of the 1980s.

In this period, I came to know not only the presidents and leading politicians of the country, but also major figures from the fields of business, science and culture. Later, when I often travelled around America giving lectures and speeches, I met many ordinary citizens and listened to what they had to say. I became well acquainted with the country and once joked that I hoped the US presidents got to see at least as many states as I had – it was more than thirty, from North Dakota to Florida and California to Massachusetts.

I like Americans; they are open and forthright, hard-working and determined. I remember how one of them wrote a letter to the editor of a local newspaper: 'I traveled several hours from a neighboring state to hear Mikhail Gorbachev's speech. I don't agree with everything he said, but he's an honest man who believes in what he does, and I trust him.' I suspect this description also applies to the author of the letter. You can get along well with people like this and eventually find common ground with them.

In contrast to some US politicians who seem to be taken with the 'arrogance of power' and interventionism, most ordinary Americans understand that their country should focus above all on its internal affairs and that their country, too, needs to change.

I recall being impressed by a question asked by a participant at an event with an audience of thousands. It was 2007, the terrorist attacks of 11 September 2001 were still very present in everyone's mind, and the citizens had rallied around their president. As people in other countries do in such situations, the American people closed ranks in the face of terrorism. And yet, at some point, many of them started to wonder: is it possible to blame every single problem on an external threat?

'Something isn't right in our country', a young man said, and then he asked me: 'What advice would you give us?'

I tried to get out of it by joking that it was the Americans who usually liked telling others what to do. But then another man stood up and asked me the same question. Of course, answering such questions requires a measure of tact and even caution. But I felt I must not evade the question. So I answered: 'I would certainly not presume to advise you on specific issues, as you would know better than I do. But it seems to me that America needs a change. America needs its own perestroika – an American-style perestroika.' The audience responded with a standing ovation.

Encounters like this taught me that most Americans do not want an empire. The idea of leadership is firmly anchored in their minds; every one of them wants to be a leader in one way or another. Yet they also have respect for the law, for other people, for their rights and their dignity. I think that both ordinary people and many important public figures are aware of the difference between imperial ambitions and true leadership. And whenever I asked people – privately or sometimes speaking to large audiences – whether they wanted America to be an empire, they would always say no.

The USA could take on a true leading role in the resolution of conflicts, the fight to save the environment and the solution of other global problems if it sought partnership instead of insisting on dominance. But the past decades have shown that American politicians have not grasped this. The use of force is still their preferred argument.

Two Trends?

We often hear that there are two contradictory tendencies in US foreign policy: one realistic and one idealistic. The 'realists' are said to defend national interests, particularly the interests of business and the military, while the 'idealists' push for democracy and human rights. This is obviously a gross simplification. It is not possible to identify two separate 'camps' in American politics. However, I would say that there is a tendency for every US administration to interpret the interests of the United States in an expansive and global way and to assert them accordingly, ignoring the interests of other countries and, recently, often to the displeasure of their allies.

Can this change? Will America find a place in the global world where it can realize its enormous potential and its economic, scientific and technological achievements without infringing on the role and interests of other countries?

This will be a key issue in world politics in the years to come. And it is not new.

I addressed this topic in my conversations with Ronald Reagan and George Bush and their secretaries of state George Schultz and James Baker. We were in agreement on many things. In the summer of 1991, I spoke with George Bush in Novo-Ogaryovo, near Moscow, about the prospects for serious cooperation between the United States and the reformed Soviet Union in order to channel global processes in a constructive direction.

This opportunity to further strengthen cooperation between the two world powers was squandered by the coup in August 1991, which was organized by a reactionary group in my own country calling itself the State Committee on the State of Emergency. The coup failed, but it weakened the position of the president of the USSR and opened the door to those who wanted to gain a personal advantage from the disintegration of the Soviet Union.

After the breakup of the USSR, the USA pursued a strategy of domination, exploiting the 'unipolar moment' solely in its own interests. Moreover, it discovered such interests in the most diverse locations on the planet: Iraq, the Balkans, Afghanistan, Libya, Syria and more recently in Venezuela. Every US president has had a war of his own.

Is the world better for it? Have ordinary American citizens benefited from these US military campaigns? Has any of this made the world safer? How long will it take to clear the rubble produced by these ventures and the ballooning military budget?

These questions must be answered by the Americans themselves. They elect their president and their congressional representatives. But the rest of the world should not just stand by and watch. Much will depend on the policy pursued by the allies of the USA and other countries, and on their negotiating partners.

I want to note one more thing here. For all the criticism

and even outrage triggered by many US actions, the important role of the United States remains undisputed, and everywhere – in Europe, China, India, Russia, Latin America – there is a willingness to cooperate with the USA. The crucial question is: is America itself willing to cooperate? And if so, on what basis: the old one or a new one?

The current phase of US policy reveals the triumph of those who are convinced that only dominance and a unilateral approach can guarantee a leading role in world politics.

But the global balance of power is changing. What's more, people are ever more staunchly rejecting the use of force to solve problems, including global ones. Sooner or later American politicians will have to acknowledge this.

We have already seen signs that the destructive attitude of the USA can be countered by policies aimed at preserving what has been achieved through the joint efforts of the international community. What we need is determination, flexibility, a clear vision of the goal and commitment to democratic methods of solving problems.

In recent times, a serious conflict has been raging around the nuclear deal with Iran. The agreement, reached in 2015, was the outcome of lengthy, painstaking negotiations between Iran and the five permanent members of the UN Security Council, plus Germany. We should give credit to all who participated in the negotiations, including the United States and, of course, Iran. It is an agreement that benefits everyone. The halt on the production of nuclear material that can be used for military purposes is still being monitored by inspectors from the International Atomic Energy Agency, who have confirmed that Iran continues to comply with the provisions.

This deal should be celebrated as a diplomatic victory for having found a good compromise despite all obstacles. But Donald Trump has undone all of this. Not only did he announce, in May 2018, that the USA was withdrawing from the agreement, without offering any convincing arguments for doing so, he also stated that the US would impose sanctions against countries and companies maintaining relations with Iran. It is unsurprising that the world viewed this decision as a manifestation of wilfulness, a betrayal of the nuclear non-proliferation arrangements.

The White House was apparently surprised by the response of many countries. Iran did not descend into hysteria; it has shown restraint and has not abandoned the monitoring regime. Despite US sanctions, the countries of the European Union have created a mechanism for maintaining trade and economic relations with Iran. Russia and China, too, have declared that they would not end their cooperation with Iran.

There is thus reason to believe that the destructive step taken by the US administration will not lead to a catastrophe in the region, which is explosive enough as it is.

Will this be a lesson to US strategists? It is still difficult to say. On this issue, the USA has actually pitted itself against the entire international community. I hope that this community will remain calm and steadfast.

A prudent, coordinated approach by all countries wanting to prevent a new arms race is also called for in connection with the US withdrawal from the agreement on interme-diate- and shorter-range missiles. Russia responded to this in a balanced and restrained manner. President Vladimir Putin declared that Russia will not be the first to deploy such weapons in Europe. It appears that most European countries do not intend to make their territory available for the deployment of American missiles. It is possible, therefore, that a new missile crisis on the European continent can be prevented. There is hope that the political leadership of the USA will learn its lesson. But it will be a struggle.

The Multipolar World Is a Reality

Americans must accept that the United States is not the only political and economic pole in the world. A multipolar world is already a reality. On issues of security, trade and migration, the US government acts as though it has the sole privilege of making decisions that others must simply acknowledge. Allies are expected to acquiesce, and partners to set aside their own interests. But this policy has repeatedly failed in the past few years.

The European Union has not abandoned the construction of the Nord Stream 2 natural gas pipeline. Turkey stated that the purchase of Russian air defence systems was a done deal. Mexico will not pay for the border wall that the US president wants to build. Other states have refused to support the decision of the US government to move its embassy in Israel to Jerusalem and to recognize the Golan Heights as Israeli territory.

The US decision to pull out of the Paris climate agreement was nearly universally condemned. The country repeatedly finds itself isolated in international organizations and is turning away from them instead of reconsidering its policies.

Can the US administration succeed in reversing the process of multipolarity under the slogans of 'Make America Great Again' and 'America First'? It does not look like it. The share of the world economy held by other countries, particularly China and India, is growing, while that of the United States has not returned to its previous level since the collapse of 2008–11.

The fact is that multipolarity best meets the demands of the modern world. These include the need to solve global problems, preserve cultural diversity, democratize international relations and embrace competition among different models of social and economic development. All of this is simply imperative in today's interdependent world.

The world does not need a 'Washington consensus', it needs a common, global understanding of the most important problems of our time. Everyone can contribute to this, from the smallest oceanic island nations to the largest continental countries.

Europe: Our Continent, Our Home

What role will Europe play? What will happen to our continent, to which humanity owes so much? But first, we need to answer this question: which Europe are we talking about?

At international conferences and in the media, Europe is often equated with the European Union. When I was confronted with this, I always asked: 'Aren't you confusing something – isn't everything that is not part of the EU, particularly Russia, still part of Europe?' This confusion has been less evident lately (perhaps because the EU itself has major problems), but it has not disappeared.

It is certainly true that the European Community – which later became the European Union – was tremendously important in Europe and the whole world, and it remains so to this day. In this unique association of states, Germany and France – former enemies in two terrible wars – managed to achieve rapprochement and partnership on a solid economic foundation. On top of this, more and more states have joined the union.

Part of its success is due to the cautious and gradual approach taken from the founding of the European Coal and Steel Community in 1952, through the Treaty of Rome in 1957, to the founding of the European Economic Community. After this, the community successively expanded and grew more integrated.

Political developments took place parallel to this which

ultimately brought an end to the East–West conflict. The Helsinki process resulted in the creation of the Organization for Security and Cooperation in Europe (OSCE). The European Economic Community transformed into a political union. It was important to synchronize these developments as much as possible in order to prevent them from drifting apart.

The idea of a common European home, a unified Europe without dividing lines, is one of the most productive ideas in our shared history. It played an undeniable role in overcoming the Cold War. Developing this idea, helping it to evolve and putting it into practice should have become the unifying theme in European politics.

I am convinced that it would have helped prevent many conflicts – in the Balkans, within the European Union and in relations between Russia and its neighbours. Unfortunately, history took a different turn.

Today, Europe has become a trouble spot in world politics. How did this happen?

I have increasingly come to believe that one of the reasons can be found in the course set by the leading countries in the European Union in the early 1990s.

Back then, the EU embarked on a path of accelerated expansion in response to the desire of a few countries to join the union. At the same time, the EU neglected the fact that its global positions depend on the strength of its internal structure. It emerged that neither old nor new EU members were complying with common standards in terms of the economy, social security and the fight against corruption.

As the EU expanded, its internal problems grew worse rather than diminishing, much to the displeasure of many citizens of its member states. They did not see any concrete benefit to a huge bureaucratic apparatus that is sluggish in responding to their problems and needs. Several crises, particularly the one in Greece, have made this attitude painfully clear. And since the 2016 Brexit referendum, the main question has been: how strong is the European Union today?

The hasty expansion process has also considerably strained relations between the EU and Russia. In the perestroika years, we started forming a new relationship through a trade and cooperation agreement in 1988. The Partnership and Cooperation Agreement between the EU and Russia was signed in 1994. In 2001, the EU–Russia summit took place, at which Romano Prodi, president of the European Commission, presented the idea of a common European economic space. This was followed in 2005 by an agreement concluded between Russia and the EU concerning strategic partnerships in four common spaces: economic issues, security and justice, external security, and research and education.

It seemed as though great prospects had opened up, very much in keeping with the idea of a common European house.

But these new opportunities depended on a dialogue between equals and consideration for Russian interests, particularly when it came to establishing relations with our neighbours, to whom we are bound by a complex and centuries-long shared history.

On this issue, the leaders of the European Union did not display sufficient political wisdom, nor did they have a long-term vision.

This was most apparent in the way the EU negotiated an association agreement with Ukraine. Was it not crystal clear that such an agreement touched directly on Russia's interests? Trade, economic relations, industrial cooperation – all of this is tied up in a knot of political, economic and legal problems. These should have been discussed at the negotiating table, with Russia participating as an equal. I am certain that Russia's participation would have been constructive. After all, Russia is very interested in a partnership with both the EU and Ukraine. But instead of negotiations, Russia was simply presented with a fait accompli. The result is well known.

Many people now seem to think that our continent has experienced an irreversible split. If this is the case, the damage to Europe will be tremendous. It will weaken the position of our continent in the inevitable competition between the regions of the global world, which has already begun. This would truly be the 'decline of Europe' spoken of by so many. We must not allow this to happen.

The only option I see is to return to the idea of a common house for all Europeans. We actually already live in a common house, but the inhabitants have not been getting along lately. This must change.

We must work together to close the rifts that emerged in the past decades and have recently grown deeper. The situation is so complex that it will require a practically titanic effort. And we have to start as soon as possible. To be honest, we should have started yesterday. Too bad the responsible political leaders did not have the necessary wisdom and strength to do so.

China and India:
The New Giants

Even in the late 1980s, when our main concern was putting an end to the arms race and the threat of nuclear war, it was clear that relations with the USA and leading European countries were only one part of the global agenda. I recall a conversation with US Secretary of State George Schultz, an experienced politician and diplomat, in which we discussed the growing role of China, India and other countries in the Asia-Pacific region. We both agreed that, in the future, they would be not only more independent, but also more influential.

Today, China and India are each, in their own way – with all the unique aspects of their history, culture and mentality – concerned primarily with improving the living conditions of their own citizens.

They have been remarkably successful. Extreme poverty is decreasing, hundreds of millions of people have been lifted out of it, and the proportion of people living in towns and in relative comfort is increasing. They are not the only ones benefiting; the economy, too, is experiencing a tremendous upswing and is aiming ever higher. None of this has been achieved by following some 'standard model'. Instead, both countries, as well as the countries of southeast Asia, chose their own path of social and economic development. This is another example of the importance of diversity and freedom of choice in a global world.

When I visited China in 1989 to end the phase of mutual

alienation and move towards cooperation and partnership, the reforms in China had just started bearing fruit and the country was going through a difficult moment in its history. Mass demonstrations by students took place before our eyes on Tiananmen Square, and their dissatisfaction was shared by other groups. The crisis came to a painful end; blood was shed. But China continued down its route of reform and opening. The country has become the workbench of the world, and its economic growth is stable and high.

China has made great strides in the areas of education, science, technology and innovation. The country became the world market leader in new patents, and it overtook the USA in educating natural scientists and engineers. One of the world's most powerful supercomputers was developed in China, and the country has made the leap into space.

There are problems nonetheless: the unequal distribution of wealth, the gap between city and country, acute environmental issues, a shortage of water. Both the Chinese themselves and the whole world have an interest in solving these problems so that China continues to grow. Of course, no country develops in a linear way, there are setbacks and even crises, but I do think China will move forward.

How will relations develop between China as a world power and other countries, including its neighbours, Russia, Japan and the USA?

During the Cold War, the question was similar but it was played out 'on a grand chess board' as a geopolitical game in which there had to be winners and losers. Since the US administration viewed China as a potential ally (or at least partner) in the confrontation with the USSR, the country was granted access to world markets, and consideration was given to its foreign policy interests. Even more recently, some US strategists, such as Zbigniew Brzezinski, have proposed a kind of American-Chinese condominium.

But in the course of overcoming the Cold War, it became clear that such geopolitical games had no prospect of success.

I remember a discussion with then US Vice-President George Bush on the relationship with China in December 1987. We agreed that it was important not to strive for one-sided advantages in relations with this huge country, and that the successful development of China and good relations between China, the USA and the Soviet Union were in everyone's interest. After all, China would act first and foremost for the benefit of its population, to defend its national interests as defined by Beijing.

I think this still applies today. The world has changed massively in the past decades, there have been tectonic shifts, but certain constants will shape the global world of tomorrow, too.

India will also play a growing role. Not everyone has noticed, but India has found its recipe for success, with economic reforms and an annual GDP growth rate of 6–8 per cent. Despite ongoing population growth, the per capita GDP continues to rise. India has developed into a world leader in information technology and successful high-tech sectors such as the nuclear industry, aerospace, telecommunications, biotechnology and pharmacy.

I am pleased that, together with Rajiv Gandhi, we laid the foundation for cooperation between our countries in these and other areas. Political understanding between our countries is just as important. The Delhi Declaration on the Principles of a Nuclear Weapon Free and Non-Violent World from 1986 is still relevant today. India is a nuclear power in the centre of a turbulent region. It is acting with restraint and a sense of responsibility.

There Is No Periphery

The fact that there is no longer any periphery in world politics probably first dawned on us in 1997–8 with the financial and economic crisis that started in Indonesia and Thailand and spread beyond the countries in the Asia-Pacific region. The shock was felt first in China, India, South Korea and Vietnam and then literally all around the world. The outflow of capital due to the crisis and the collapse in commodity prices impacted countries as different and distant from Asia as Russia and Argentina. We in Russia have still not forgotten the rouble crisis of August 1998, when the state was unable to settle its debts and the rouble collapsed for the second time in the space of barely ten years.

Since the world economy is interconnected, something similar may well happen again. But globalization offers more than just risks. We should think of the countries that seized the opportunities of the global market and made great advances. Examples of 'economic miracles' can be found on all continents, many of which predate the present wave of globalization. I have in mind such countries as Japan and Singapore which, in the 1950s and 1960s, were among the first to overcome immense difficulties and take leading positions in the world economy.

I was in Japan many times and honestly marvel at how the citizens of this earthquake-prone island nation with scarce natural resources have succeeded in making it flourish and become an economic giant.

Anyone who dismisses Japan today as an ageing dragon on account of its demographic problems and slower growth is making a big mistake. We must not forget how, after the cataclysm of the Second World War, this nearly devastated country created an economic miracle. Its people are benefiting from this miracle. For many decades now, Japan has been one of the countries with the longest life expectancy

– a key figure that is an important indicator of the development level of any country.

Japan remains a land of advanced technology and unique culture. Perhaps this is its secret to success. The Japanese got their national economy back on its feet and managed to transform it – not by following someone else's recipe but on the basis of their own economic strategy, which was hammered out by the state and business sector together. Above all, they took the special aspects of their nation's culture, traditions and mentality into account.

They quickly switched from metallurgy, shipbuilding and petrochemicals to electronics and the automobile industry. In the process, they created an effective infrastructure and learned to manufacture products of the highest quality.

Japan has its own economic model. Nowadays, we often hear that it has to be adapted so the country can reassert its leading role in the world economy. I am convinced that the Japanese will find their own original solution to this challenge. They will certainly not rush ahead of themselves. The Japanese tend to seek balance and to think through every single step. This was my impression in my many discussions with citizens and members of Japan's political and business elite.

At the same time, they radiate optimism and confidence. Whenever I visited, I sensed good will and warmth towards me personally and towards the people of Russia, even though the relationship between our countries is strained by what is known as the islands dispute – that is, the issue of the southern Kuril Islands. But I note that the concept of rapprochement I proposed in the early 1990s, to focus on creating mutual trust in order to peacefully resolve this territorial problem in the future, appears to be gaining ground today.

Malaysia is another example of economic success according to the principle of 'following your own mind'. Malaysia's political leadership has repeatedly rejected the prescriptions of the International Monetary Fund and other financial institutions and has charted a successful course on its own.

The growth rate is higher in Malaysia than in the neighbouring countries referred to as 'Asian tigers'. Thanks to its improved standard of living, Malaysia can no longer be regarded as a third world country. There have been crises and economic shocks, but they have generally been overcome more quickly here than elsewhere.

I mention all these examples not because I hold them up as perfect solutions, but because I am confident that every country can find its own path to prosperity and success by drawing on its own intellectual potential, taking the experiences of others into account and creating favourable external conditions.

This is not the case everywhere, of course. Many countries in Africa and Latin America, for example, face major obstacles. Yet it would be wrong to assume that they are doomed to be left behind in the global economic space. Their time, too, will come.

The Middle East: Tense Hub of World Politics

Perpetual conflicts always pose a danger of new clashes and convulsions. The most explosive region in this respect is the Middle East, viewed by many as the powder keg of the world.

This huge conflict region, which extends to the countries of North Africa, is particularly unstable.

We need only think of the assassination of Pakistani Prime Minister Benazir Bhutto, the failed military coup in Turkey, the Arab Spring that took off rapidly in Tunisia, Egypt and Syria and then stalled, the American invasion of Iraq, the deployment of foreign armed forces in Libya and Syria, and the continued pressure placed on Iran by the USA.

This turbulence has many internal causes, but it is exacerbated by external factors. At the centre of it all, of course, is the decades-long Arab–Israeli conflict. A careful look reveals that many of the problems in this region and the world community as a whole, including the migration crisis, can be traced back to this conflict.

Why has no resolution been found? After all, it was on the basis of the coexistence of two states – Israel and the State of Palestine – that we came close to finding solutions multiple times that would have been acceptable to both sides, with Israel's neighbours officially recognizing Israel.

I remember the Madrid Middle East Peace Conference that began in October 1991. This step was possible after the USSR and the USA adopted a unified position against Iraq's invasion of Kuwait. A formula was found that enabled Israel and the Palestinians to sit down together at the negotiating table. The first agreement between Israel and the PLO was signed in Washington, DC, in 1993. Yitzhak Rabin, Shimon Peres and Yasser Arafat received the Nobel Peace Prize for this. But it was not possible to follow up on these successes. The region gradually sank back into confrontation and hostility.

I cannot say that the international community and major powers did nothing to change this. Serious attempts were made, particularly by the quartet of mediators (the USA, Russia, the UN and the EU) to develop a road map to peace in the Middle East. They did not succeed, however, and new eruptions of violence in the region later negated the effect of the mediation efforts. Lethargy now dominates any ambition to pursue a peace settlement for the Middle East.

Meanwhile, external interventions in countries such as Iraq, Libya and Syria have disrupted their lives for years to come, thus creating new obstacles to a peaceful solution.

In recent years, countries in the region have increasingly acted with no regard for either world opinion or the position of the major nations whose influence they previously acknowledged and whose views they valued. This has given rise to new dividing lines and political schemes that pose a great danger.

If we continue to resign ourselves to stagnation in the Middle East, we run the risk of allowing new outbreaks of violence and internal destabilization in several countries, which will promote terrorism and trigger new waves of 'migration. We must not be under any illusions: neither walls nor fences will help here.

The Islamic World

Islamic civilization will occupy an important place in the future world order. At the start of the twentieth century, around 150 million people – almost a tenth of the world's population – professed the Islamic faith. Today, it is 1.7 billion, nearly a quarter of humanity all around the world.

Some people think the root cause of many of today's problems lies in the nature of Islam, which supposedly goes against the values of the modern world and encourages violence. This is utterly wrong. Basing policy on Islamophobia means setting yourself against hundreds of millions of people.

I have a question for those who want to embark on a 'crusade' against the Muslim world and its religion under the banner of fighting extremism. What do you want to do to the people who are sincerely committed to the centuries-old faith of their fathers and forefathers? Punish them, 're-educate' them, Westernize them?

Not every country dominated by Islam has been able to master the main trends of the modern world. These countries, particularly in the Arab world, face great difficulties in adjusting to the challenges of globalization. But this has nothing to do with some 'inherent flaw' (which is a widespread notion, unfortunately) and everything to do with historical circumstances.

The Islamic world is in the midst of a difficult phase of development. After flourishing in the Middle Ages, it was pushed to the margins of history. Over the course of centuries, others decided its fate. But it is impossible to deny the contributions that Islamic civilization has made to the development of culture, philosophy and the natural sciences – algebra, astronomy, chemistry.

Islam expanded to encompass vast regions, from Spain to Indonesia, and everywhere it left behind evidence of a unique material and artistic culture. The golden age of Islamic civilization from the ninth to the twelfth century produced many inventions and discoveries that continue to benefit all of humanity today.

Later, the Reformation, the Renaissance, the Age of Discovery and, ultimately, the Industrial Revolution enabled West European civilization to break through and become the centre of scientific, technical and cultural progress. But we know full well just how difficult and painful this process was. The brutality of colonialism and early capitalism, militarism that plunged Europe into two world wars, slavery in the southern United States – all these 'birthmarks' of Western civilization continue to reverberate around the world today.

We cannot approach the Islamic world with a feeling of superiority; we must interact with it and try to understand it in all its complexity and contradictions.

These contradictions are so deeply rooted that we cannot speak of a conflict of cultures, but rather of conflicts within this culture. They have their origins both in the history of Islam and in current developments.

The conflict between Sunnis and Shiites has lasted for a millennium and a half, and the followers of both denominations believe that only their own teaching speaks the truth. This defines the rivalry between two major countries in the Islamic world: Saudi Arabia and Iran.

There is great strife between the different ideological and political currents: traditionalists, moderates (including democratic reformists), and radicals or jihadists who have chosen the path of violence and terror.

Although the radicals have been curbed recently, it is clear that they will not be defeated by military means alone.

The fight against extremism in the Islamic world must be a political and ideological fight above all. We must push back against those who preach hate and violence, while we also seek dialogue with moderate Islamists. And we must include Islamic states and movements in political processes. At the same time, we should recognize the emergence of secular movements and forces in these countries that could eventually challenge dictators and religious extremists.

What Must Not Happen

The Greater Middle East (that is, the Middle East plus North Africa) is a region now beset by many contradictions and bloody conflicts. Waves of migration and the modern media carry these conflicts around the world, particularly to Europe.

There is a danger that they will fan the flames of strife between different cultures and religions. We must not close our eyes to this. We must do all we can to avert this threat.

It is important to realize that a fatal clash of cultures is not inevitable. Nations are not hostile towards one another on account of their traditional cultures. Not a single major religion, holy text or god calls upon the devout to commit senseless violence.

This is not a conflict between different cultures, it is a conflict between civilization and barbarity. Extremists, fanatics, fundamentalist ideologues and, unfortunately, also irresponsible politicians are stoking hate between people.

Why has this situation grown so dire in recent decades?

Here, too, we have to talk about globalization. In its present form, it often equates to destabilization. Globalization hits weaker countries particularly hard, especially developing countries and transitional societies, and it makes the continued existence of cultural diversity in the world even more difficult. The gap between prosperity and poverty, the fight for markets and access to sources of energy and other natural resources, the informational and cultural expansion of the West, which is perceived by others as a threat to their cultural identity – all of this breeds national and religious fundamentalism, ethnic separatism and xenophobia.

When politics, the media and public opinion do not counter this, these feelings are exploited by extremists, terrorists and authoritarian regimes, undermining internal peace and threatening international stability.

Humanity is facing a serious challenge. How can we make it possible for different cultures and religions to peacefully coexist and enrich one another? Political and spiritual leaders and the society as a whole must seek an answer to this question.

The Arab Spring that began in 2011 showed how arduous their struggle is going to be.

The Rollback of Democracy

Historians speak of three 'long waves' of democratization. Both the first wave, which ended after the First World War, and the second, which began in the 1960s, were followed by periods of rollback. Authoritarian, dictatorial and totalitarian regimes returned to the world stage. The third wave, which was accelerated by perestroika in the Soviet Union and the end of the Cold War, was no exception to this. At the start of the twenty-first century, scholars noted a turnaround in the trend towards democratization, as well as growing pessimism regarding the future of democracy. Political scientists do not rule out the possibility that the twenty-first century will see a revival of authoritarianism.

It is true that there are only a few remaining dictatorial regimes worldwide that openly and systematically suppress the rights and freedoms of their citizens (and even they often disguise themselves with democratic slogans). However, the number of 'hybrid' regimes, or countries in which democratic institutions are merely imitated, is on the rise.

Instead of expanding, democratic institutions in these countries are slowly being strangled as a way of neutralizing political opposition, recalcitrant media and an independent judiciary. Europe is sadly familiar with this model from its fairly recent history, and we know where it can lead in its extreme form. All of this often happens with the tacit approval of the public. Over the course of years, one becomes accustomed to such a state, and elections become a formality – with predetermined results favouring the powers that be.

Some think that, since social processes are subject to fluctuation, with revolutions almost always followed by counter-revolutions and reforms by counter-reforms, a new wave of democratization is practically inevitable.

As much as we may want this to be the case, it is at best half true.

I am extremely concerned by current anti-democratic tendencies. What exactly has happened? First and foremost, many people are disappointed by the results of the democratic process and the politicians who came to power under the banner of democracy. Surveys show that this is the case even in countries with longstanding democratic traditions. Sociologists have identified 'democracy fatigue' even among young people. No wonder it is found in countries that are just starting to acquire democratic processes and learning how to live and think in a democratic way.

When our neighbours – the peoples of Central and Eastern Europe – expressed their desire for democracy and freedom at the end of the 1980s, the leadership of the Soviet Union did not stand in their way. This was largely because we ourselves had chosen this path.

In Russia, I am still accused of having 'given away' Eastern Europe. My response to this is: who did I give it away to? Poland to the Poles, Hungary to the Hungarians, Czechoslovakia to the Czechs and Slovaks! I remain firmly convinced that we did what was right back then.

Largely for this reason, the velvet revolutions in these countries were nonviolent and bloodless. The citizens placed high expectations on the new politicians in power, but far from all of them were fulfilled. Despite painful economic reforms, most countries in this region still trail behind those in the West in terms of standards of living and quality of life. The global economic crisis of 2008 laid bare the shortcomings of the transformation process, and it intensified citizens' disaffection with corruption and the alienation of the powerful from the problems of the people. This disaffection is also directed at the structures of the European Union, regarded by a growing number of people as an undemocratic and bureaucratic superstructure.

Who Is Undermining Faith in Democracy?

Another reason for the ebbing of the democratic wave and faltering trust in democracy can be found in the policies of those countries considered to be leaders in terms of socio-economic development, the establishment of democratic institutions and the promotion of the rights and freedoms of their citizens. Above all, this means the countries of Western Europe and the USA.

Their role in the world community goes hand in hand with a special responsibility. And if they want to take a leading role in the promotion of democracy, their own domestic and foreign policy must meet the highest democratic standards.

I regularly told our Western partners, particularly American politicians, that it was impossible to impose democracy; it cannot be transported to other countries and continents like sachets of instant coffee, let alone by means of tanks and troop carriers. It is time to abandon attempts to force democracy on others and grant people the freedom to make their own choice, one that aligns with their culture, mentality and tradition.

I have to say that Western politicians did not follow this advice. They claimed the right – and virtually declared it their mission – to assign grades for democracy, to indict countries and peoples, take them to court, convict them and carry out the sentence.

What else would you call the military actions in Yugoslavia, Iraq and Libya? They each took place under different pretences, but they were always accompanied by 'democratic' rhetoric.

If we are to evaluate the degree of democracy in developed countries, we should not do so on the basis of formal criteria alone. Elections, changes of power, free media and human rights are important indicators, of course. But have all these things been fully realized in the countries with a 'stable democracy'? Why are the signs of public dissatisfaction growing on a massive scale? Would it not be better to focus on these problems?

After all, nothing discredits democracy more than the failure of democratic politicians to find solutions to problems that affect the people.

If no lessons are learned from the latest failures of the West in foreign policy and the resolution of domestic problems, if there is no democratization of democracy, then competing political models will become increasingly attractive to many people. I fear that we are approaching this line. It would be dangerous to cross it.

The Responsibility of the Media

The media are partially responsible for the problems of modern democracy, but I do not want to start by criticizing the media.

I have great respect for the printed press and new electronic media alike, and I value the work of journalists. I have always viewed them as the most important mediators between politics and society, as a source of ideas and catalyst for change.

It is no coincidence that we launched the reforms in our country with glasnost – freedom of expression and of the press. We gave people the chance to talk about their worries without fear. My fellow countryman Alexander Solzhenitsyn was wrong when he said 'Gorbachev's glasnost ruined everything'. Without glasnost, no reforms would have begun, and even if they had begun, they would have been stifled, as had often happened in the past.

Journalists increasingly face risks in their work. They often go from being observers to witnesses to targets of political repression, hostages and victims of dictatorships, civil wars and international conflicts. We owe our respect to all those who have lost their lives in war zones at the hands of terrorists, corrupt officials and other enemies of freedom. Some of them were friends of mine, people who had rebuilt the Russian press.

Whenever I saw journalists being attacked, threatened or put under pressure, I defended them and tried to help them.

There is no denying the courage and professionalism of most of them, and their services to democracy.

But we also have to talk about the problems and dilemmas of modern journalism. We exist today in a new global information environment, with a growing concentration of media and competition from the internet, social media and a wide variety of channels for distributing information. How these new resources are affecting the quality of information has not yet been fully studied. One thing is clear, however: in light of the rapid development of new technologies, growing demands are being placed on the media and journalists in terms of professionalism, morality and responsibility.

This is the technological aspect. There are two other influencing factors, however. The interplay between politics and economics (particularly big business) and the media is a complex and especially urgent issue today. The fact is that there is dissatisfaction in society with the view of reality portrayed by the modern media. More and more people are starting to harbour the doubts expressed by Russian director Stanislavski in his famous words to his actors: 'I don't believe you!'

The blurring of the line between objective information and subjective opinion, examples of open and concealed censorship including self-censorship, superficial reporting, a confusing wealth of pseudo-information with accompanying silence regarding truly important events, the phenomenon of invented, falsified news ('fake news'), hysterical talk shows that take the place of serious discussion and goad their participants in every imaginable way, advertising that overloads electronic and print media alike – these phenomena are not new, but in the past decades they have caused the media to increasingly reflect a distorted image of reality. Who benefits from this?

First and foremost, the cynical and unprincipled owners of many media. The process of media monopolization is in full swing in many countries. Newspapers as well as radio and television broadcasters are in the hands of businesspeople who want to maximize profits above all. This is the main reason the quality of many newspapers, magazines and television stations has declined so severely. Worst of all, this affects the people themselves. They turn their back on politics, become less interested in information and merely seek confirmation of their beliefs while rejecting out of hand opinions that deviate from theirs.

This problem is even more acute in social media. It appears that many active social media users and popular bloggers who have direct access to millions of followers are not aware of their responsibility. Even aside from cases of actual criminal liability (incitement of violence and terrorism or participation in the formation of criminal associations, etc.), society has many reasons to call them to account. Stop fomenting hate, promoting ignorance and destroying political culture!

I know that censorship or erecting walls and fences on the internet is not the way to solve this problem. It appears that opinion leaders, governments and leading social media networks have recently become concerned about this issue. The challenge has been acknowledged, but there is still no solution. I propose that our search for a balance between freedom and responsibility must be based on the moral criteria and standards that have evolved over centuries. They are not outdated, but they do need to be adapted to modern life.

Civil Society and International Organizations

Civil society has become aware of its rights and influence in most countries today. Thanks to the activities of citizens and their organizations, individuals are no longer left to their own devices if they have to defend their right to a dignified life against the state or an employer.

But, of course, civil society in different countries operates under different conditions and with different results.

There are still many countries in which civil activists are persecuted. Just like journalists, these people often courageously risk their lives. They deserve our support and our protection.

Those governments that believe they can ensure stability for years and decades to come by oppressing civil society are deeply misguided. On the contrary, their actions set their countries back by decades and rob them of sources of initiative and progress.

Over the years, I have met with hundreds of representatives of social movements and nongovernmental organizations all over the world. These people dedicate their lives to the common good, and their commitment encompasses the entire global agenda: nuclear disarmament, environmental protection, fighting poverty, protecting fundamental rights and freedoms, equal rights for people with disabilities and much more.

So many people invest all their energy in humanitarian and charitable projects! I worked alongside some of them, including in Russia, where we managed to make great strides in the treatment of childhood leukaemia, for example.

I have no doubt that social movements have a great future. A global civil society will gradually emerge and new transnational communities will develop, as is already happening among scientists, human rights defenders and environmentalists.

The international protest movement against the arms race once played a major role in getting the process of nuclear disarmament off the ground. Millions of people took to the streets, engaged in people-to-people democracy, voiced their demands, found a common language – and politicians in the East and West finally responded.

At the same time, the world was shaken by the famines in Africa, particularly in Ethiopia and Sudan. People around the world heeded the call of activists, musicians and actors to help the victims of the environmental disasters there. The song 'We Are the World' is a hymn to this truly brotherly support.

Today, too, millions of people in a similarly powerful movement should raise their voices for peace and disarmament in the world.

A global civil society will be created if we respect one another and show consideration for our differences. I say this both to the politicians and to the activists in social movements: every country and every society must mature in its own way economically, politically and psychologically so as to absorb new ideas and trends that are initially unfamiliar.

If, however, people feel that ideas and trends are being forced upon them, it has exactly the opposite effect.

The most difficult problem for the global world of the future will be to ensure sensible governance. It is not yet clear what this will look like, but a 'world government' is the wrong route to take.

The existing institutions of the world community, particularly the United Nations and its organizations, have come under a lot of criticism. They have been accused of weakness and inefficiency. But the United Nations will always be as strong and effective as its member states want it to be. This is why it is necessary to push seriously for the democratization of international organizations. They should be more open and transparent for public control and more responsive to the needs of ordinary citizens. The leading bodies of these organizations should be more representative and pluralistic. And the people directly affected by decisions should have a say in them.

The New Russia

Russia is my home and the only country in which I can imagine living. When I think about the world of the future, I am confident that Russia can make a major positive contribution to it.

In its thousand-year history, Russia has seen both triumph and upheaval. The modern Russian state is the heir to Ancient Rus, the Grand Principality of Moscow, the Russian Empire and the Soviet era. Today, like all countries, Russia is in the process of finding its place in the future global world. Russian society is still in a transitional phase – from totalitarianism and lack of freedom to democracy. Such a transition cannot be easy.

Both in the Soviet era and in the Russia of today, this process has been complicated by the fact that the Russian state has been multinational and multilayered for centuries, with dozens of nationalities and ethnic groups. The constitution of the USSR declared the Soviet republics to be sovereign states with the right to secede from the Union – but this was sovereignty on paper alone. In fact, the USSR was a strictly centralized unitary state.

Perestroika and freedom of expression fired up the people, and the republics demanded more autonomy and some of them even independence.

I firmly believed that the only way for the republics to be politically sovereign, economically independent and in a position to develop their own identity and culture was to

fundamentally modernize the Union. This meant trans-
forming it into a real, democratic and effectively organized
federation to which the individual republics would delegate
part of their powers. The decisive step in this direction would
have been the new Union Treaty, the signing of which was
prevented by the coup carried out by reactionary forces in
August 1991.

As president, I fought for the unity of the country until
the very end. I fought by political means – it is important
to emphasize this – and I tried to win over Soviet citizens
and my colleagues, the leaders of the Union republics. Even
today, I believe that the integrity of the country could have
been preserved and that a new Union was in everyone's
interest.

But the coup weakened my position, and the leadership of
Russia, the largest republic of the USSR, under Boris Yeltsin
decided to dissolve the Soviet Union instead. The country
fell apart, the state collapsed.

Tens of millions of people in Russia and beyond soon felt
the effects of this decision. It is no surprise that all surveys
show the majority of Russians still mourn the breakup of the
Soviet Union and look back on the 1990s as the most difficult
time. The economic chaos that ensued – because economic
ties were cut between the republics of the former Soviet
Union and overhasty reforms were pushed through – resulted
in a dramatic drop in most people's standard of living. In this
weakened condition, Russia was unable to integrate itself as a
strong power in the world economy.

All this inevitably limited its scope for foreign policy.
Russia no longer spoke with a strong voice on the world
stage, as a great power should. Many political decisions made
in the West, and in the United States above all, went against
Russia's national interests at the time, but Russia could do
nothing to counteract them and no consideration was given
to it. Russia was presented with a fait accompli.

Russia eventually freed itself from this predicament, however. In the first decade of the new millennium, the economy recovered and the country returned to the world stage to defend its own interests.

As president, Vladimir Putin inherited political and economic chaos from his predecessor. This also affected relations between Moscow and Russia's republics and regions. The government apparatus had been weakened, and the political institutions were barely functioning. In the 1990s, Russia's gross domestic product fell by nearly half. Russia was just beginning to recover from the crisis of 1998, which hit our country particularly hard and led to the government defaulting on its debt and the devaluation of the rouble.

One of the republics in the Russian Federation – Chechnya – became a breeding ground for terrorism. Many regions had enacted laws and decrees that were inconsistent with federal law. The Russian state was beginning to disintegrate, as were the army, the social sector, the economy and the sciences.

Under these circumstances, democracy by the book could not bring an end to the catastrophic situation. History had simply not given us enough time for this. The president's only option was to act decisively. Parts of society responded critically to his steps, some of which were perceived as authoritarian. The mass media were placed under intense state pressure. To protect the integrity of the state and eliminate the hotbed of terrorism, it was necessary to use military force in Chechnya. Efforts were also made to align regional legislation with federal legislation.

The actions taken by the central government in Moscow were not always entirely appropriate. The weakened role of parliament and the judiciary, the creation of a 'power vertical' at the expense of regional self-government, and the state's expansion of control over electronic media – all of this was viewed critically. But the people soon realized that things were gradually changing for the better.

I was often asked at the time how I felt about the authoritarian elements in the actions of the Russian authorities. I was not blind to them, but I thought it would be wrong to judge the president's policies on this basis alone. It is necessary to consider the circumstances in which he was forced to act. And if the government's goal was to create the conditions for a strong, modern democracy, I was prepared to support the president even if I did not agree with some of his decisions.

The country's leadership was confronted with an extremely difficult socioeconomic situation. The financial collapse in August 1998 had nearly halved the real income of Russia's citizens. The country was insolvent. Leading commercial banks had broken apart. The measures that were taken made it possible to stop the crisis from spreading, stabilize the economy and create conditions for recovery.

But the Russian government was unable to end the domestic economy's dependence on commodity exports. I have also criticized other aspects of the government's economic policy, particularly the attempt to limit social benefits for pensioners, which led to mass protests. However, it must be acknowledged that in the first decade of the new century, the standard of living for millions of Russians improved considerably, leading to a rise in real income. The economic chaos of the 1990s was consigned to the past.

Setting the Course in Foreign Policy

I have already described how Russia was too weak after the collapse of the USSR to make a clear decision on what direction its foreign policy should take. While the USA strove for a unipolar world, Russia responded hesitantly to events and challenges that directly touched on its interests.

Russian foreign policy had no effective strategy or clear understanding of our national interests. This became very apparent at the turn of the century, when Vladimir Putin took office. While there was near unanimity in both Russia and many other countries that a unipolar world harboured great dangers, Putin emphasized that Russia recognized the role of the West, and the USA above all, in world politics and the world economy. Russia took several steps that accommodated the West. Putin was the first head of state to call the US president directly after the terrorist attacks of 11 September 2001. He offered wide-ranging support in the fight against terrorism and opened Russian airspace for deliveries of military goods to Afghanistan. Russia was ready for a partnership with the West, including with NATO. Russia was also willing to be flexible on issues in dispute, provided its own interests were taken into account.

Neither then nor later did Russia's foreign policy proclaim the goals often attributed to it. Russia never sought the 'rebirth of the empire', 'zones of influence' or geopolitical expansion. But even Russia's natural interest in integration processes with its neighbours and closer cooperation with the members of the Commonwealth of Independent States (CIS) was met with distrust and sometimes open pushback from the West. Our Western partners also failed to appreciate the initiative of then-president Dmitry Medvedev in 2008 to create a new Europe-wide security system reinforced by consultation and conflict-prevention mechanisms.

In general, it must be said that Russia's attempt at constructive interaction was not acknowledged by the West. The Western leaders did not show a real willingness for dialogue or for accommodating Russia on issues of vital importance to it. These included the enlargement of NATO, the problems of strategic stability and missile defence, trade and economic relations and Europe's energy supply. Every step Russia took was eyed suspiciously by the West, and it was unjustly accused of wanting to revive the Soviet Union and take geopolitical revenge.

Russia had much more reason to criticize its Western partners, as President Putin finally did at the Munich Security Conference in February 2007.

Re-reading this speech now, I do not see the grounds for the Western criticism of it. It does not exhibit an anti-American, anti-Western or uncooperative attitude, it is not aggressive, and it is certainly not a 'declaration of a new Cold War', as some people claimed. On the contrary, I find in it much that any sensible person must agree with.

Is it wrong to assert that a unipolar model for the modern world is not only unacceptable but not viable? That the UN Charter is the only mechanism for approving the use of military force as a last resort? That it is necessary to find a balance between different national interests? That no state may force its own legal system on another state? Those are the points Putin made in his Munich speech, and I do not see how one can object to them.

In Munich, Vladimir Putin declared that Russia would in future pursue an independent foreign policy. No one could seriously argue with this. This is the choice Russia made. It is final, and it will have to be reckoned with.

Thinking about the Future

No one is now saying that Russia can be written off or that it has no prospects for the future. A great deal has been achieved in the first two decades of this century, and a new generation has become active in politics and the economy. Russia can stand proud – but there are several things to consider.

What prospects does the Russian state offer its citizens? Which political system do we want? What type of economic order? And the main question, perhaps, is: what should Russian society look like?

These questions remain largely unanswered.

The political system has developed primarily on the basis of the constitution of 1993, and its balance is tipped in favour of the executive and presidential power, to the detriment of the legislature. Furthermore, changes in electoral legislation and procedures have meant that parliamentarians are less accountable to the citizens. And the electoral system in the regions, regional parliaments and municipal administrations is not exactly designed to identify and promote the best and brightest.

Russia's political parties still have no cohesive, convincing programmes. Russian politicians seem to have forgotten that parties are not formed by decree from above – they have to grow from below. The United Russia Party, which relies above all on the apparatus of state, has never become a real political party with convincing ideas and a serious programme. The other parties represented in parliament are not much more than decoration, and many parties are prevented from entering parliament at all.

All of this is taking place in the name of stability. We do need stability, but it must be based on democratic principles, dialogue and open competition between responsible political currents and parties. We have not yet achieved this; at best, we are only halfway there. But we must not let up, otherwise we will lose time and face the possibility of failure.

Equally important for Russia is the question of a regular change of government. This must be enshrined in law. According to the constitution of 1993, the president's time in office is limited to two terms in succession. But this allows for the possibility of taking a break after two terms and being elected again, so there is practically no limitation. Vladimir Putin was thus able to run for office once more following the presidency of Dmitry Medvedev (2008–12). He was subsequently elected president for two terms of six years each.

Putin's popularity and high standing among the population are real, as are his services to Russian society. This has to do with his personal qualities: he is smart, strong-willed and hard-working. The people appreciate the positive changes they have experienced in their life under Putin. Many of them believe they must hold on to the president if they do not want to lose what they have attained.

But does it make sense for political processes and decisions to continue to be geared towards a single person? What could be the cost of a mistake in a political model such as this? And can we really expect the personal qualities of the president to always compensate for the drawbacks of this model?

The president himself should ponder these questions. We need a broad public debate about this. Of course, we cannot risk the stability of our society, for which we have fought so hard after the challenges of the 1990s. But we have to think about the future. The stability of the state and the prospects for a country's development ultimately depend on the strength of its political institutions, the people's trust in these institutions and the continual renewal brought about by fresh forces in politics. Otherwise we face inertia, stagnation and political apathy. Relatively recent history has shown just how dangerous this is.

The Economy for the People

The Russian economy has changed fundamentally since the late twentieth century; it has become an integral part of the world economy. Millions of people are now entrepreneurs, and many small and medium-sized businesses have been founded. The term 'deficit' – formerly used to refer to shortages of goods and long lines in the stores – is a thing of the past. Russia was able to create a stable macroeconomic framework with low inflation and a generally stable economy. It withstood the shockwaves unleashed by the volatility of commodity prices and Western sanctions.

But there are still many problems to be solved. Russia is not one of the leading countries in the world economy. Its growth rates have slowed, and this has affected the people's standard of living. Prime Minister Dmitry Medvedev mentioned the following figure: 19 million Russians are living below the poverty line. The years of the energy boom and rapid economic growth in the first decade of the twenty-first century were not used to diversify the economy, to stimulate it with innovations or to develop our own new technologies. There is too little competition in most sectors of the Russian economy. Other acute problems include income inequality and the gap between the big cities and less-developed regions. The fight against corruption has also not yet born much fruit.

It is obvious that an inertia scenario – meaning a continuation of the current economic course without major changes – will make it impossible to achieve economic growth above the global average, as called for by the president. New ways must be found to accelerate this growth, not just nominally but so that it benefits the people.

After his re-election in the spring of 2018, President Putin signed the 'May Decree' on the strategic development goals for the period until 2024. The goal is to achieve a breakthrough in Russia's development by implementing national projects in three main areas: human capital, quality of life and economic growth.

The president clearly wants to overcome inertia and stagnation. Specific tasks were defined in each of the areas covered by the national projects: health care, education, demography, infrastructure, ecology, housing and urban environment, small/medium enterprises and more. For the first time in Russian history, scientific research and technological development were declared a priority, a major national project. The state has earmarked substantial funding for this in the hope of also stimulating private investment.

Since 2006, Russia has had experience with implementing national priority projects under the heading of 'Investment in People'. Not all the plans from back then were realized, but the balance is generally positive. Without relying on the 'invisible hand of the market', the state initiated the technical modernization of its health care and education systems, it connected schools to the internet, stimulated housing construction and subsidized mortgage loans. Now the same approach is to be used on a much larger scale.

I am convinced that Russia has everything it needs to make great advances, not just on account of its wealth of natural resources, but above all on account of its human capital. Russia is rich in talent, and its citizens are willing to work hard. The businesspeople and investors active in Russia know this all too well. The vast majority of them stay in our country despite all the obstacles. Artificial obstacles to trade and investment must be eliminated, and I am sure that new partners will come to Russia and will not be disappointed.

Democracy and Society

Where is Russia heading? I am often asked this question at home and abroad, usually with an undertone of doubt as to whether Russia is capable of becoming a true democracy. Sometimes I am bluntly asked how the laws and decisions made by the Russian authorities are compatible with democratic principles.

I always respond that our people are more democratically minded than you might think. But Russia has had a difficult history: 250 years of the Mongol yoke, serfdom, Stalin's repressions. People were raised to believe they may be treated like slaves. When this finally ended, they were forced in the 1990s – just as democracy was emerging – to experience chaos and arbitrary rule.

Our people should learn from their past. They must learn to choose what to accept and what to reject. This takes time. But the only future for Russia is democracy.

Russian society is gradually evolving into a real civil society, a true political nation. Democracy and the creation of a functioning civil society go hand in hand. Indeed, civil society is the implementation of the most important principle of democracy: the people's involvement in political debates and decision-making processes. Bureaucracy cannot manage all of these tasks alone.

The creation of civil society is a complex process, and we have no deep-seated traditions of self-organization to draw on in Russia. This has only ever happened in times of emergency, such as during natural disasters and national tragedies.

Today, however, we need solidarity, cooperation and civil self-organization in times of peace – for the sake of building. This is a very difficult task, but it is achievable. I sense this particularly when I meet with young people.

Students are my favourite audience, and I love talking with them. I am often amazed by their openness, their intellectual independence, their curiosity and their willingness to listen. As long as my health allowed it, I travelled the country and gave lectures to all kinds of audiences, and I was always inspired to see how perestroika and glasnost had irrevocably changed people for the better.

The Russians now live in a different system of coordinates.

Perhaps I lost as a politician, perhaps my self-confidence played a trick on me because I did not recognize the double threat – from zealots and radicals, and from reactionaries in my immediate surroundings. Nonetheless, perestroika won. A relapse into the past is out of the question.

The people today are ready for alternatives, for political competition. And to the rulers in Russia, I say: Do not fear the people! Do not try to rein in social movements. Do not offer people elections without real choice, elections whose outcome has already been determined. Do not view those who demonstrate, protest or sign petitions as enemies.

A lively, creative and demanding civil society is in the interest of the citizens and government alike. I am sure that such a civil society will emerge in Russia.

Re-establish Trust

In world politics today, there is no more important or difficult task than re-establishing trust between Russia and the West. The West is well aware that this is necessary, because without Russia, none of the big global problems can be solved. And yet, responsibility for the current crisis is laid entirely at Russia's feet, and Russia is told to make one-sided concessions to the West.

Russia must not be spoken to in this way. Moreover, no one should even attempt to isolate Russia. Such attempts have utterly failed in recent years. Russia maintains close relations with dozens of countries around the world. Its role as a permanent member of the UN Security Council is generally acknowledged. Even after relations with the Western countries, and particularly the USA, had deteriorated, Russia did not shy away from working together with these countries on sensitive global policy issues. One need only think of Russia's initiative to eliminate Syria's chemical weapons under international control. This happened at a time when all signs seemed to indicate that military force would be used against Syria. Thanks to Russia, this line was never crossed.

Russia played an equally constructive role in the complicated negotiations on Iran's nuclear programme. Russia did not move a centimetre from its principled stance, and it did not try to obstruct its Western partners. As a result, an agreement was reached that, not coincidentally, bore the name 'Joint Comprehensive Plan of Action'. This shows how unity can be achieved even on the most contentious of issues. Is Russia to blame for the fact that the implementation of this plan is now more threatened than ever due to the US administration's decision?

These are just two examples. It is dishonest and irresponsible to paint Russia as the enemy always pondering how to stymie America. The first time we met, I said to Ronald Reagan: 'Mr. President, if you believe we just sit in the Kremlin and think about how we can hurt the USA, you are wrong.' I am confident that the Russian president could say the same thing today.

In a dangerous and unpredictable world, Russia has to take the necessary measures to guarantee its security. However, Russia understands that arms control, especially for nuclear weapons, is absolutely essential. It recently became known that Russia had proposed signing a joint document at the Russia–United States summit of the two presidents that would state: 'A nuclear war cannot be won and must never be fought.' This is a direct quote from the joint statement that Ronald Reagan and I adopted at our first summit in Geneva in November 1985. Back then, this was a signal to start negotiations that led to radical cuts in the nuclear arsenals. The world should support Russia's new initiative so that the next step can be to adopt this declaration on a multilateral level as well.

Relations between Russia and the West are plagued by a lack of willingness to understand one another. Our partners are not making any attempt to do so. Is it not obvious that relations with our nearest neighbours, such as Georgia and Ukraine, are objectively much more important to Russia than to any other country, the USA included, if only because we have a centuries-old bond and want to have good neighbours?

I recall how, after the conflict in Georgia that began with the use of force against South Ossetia, I wrote an article in the *Washington Post* about the history of the conflict and its causes. 'Mikheil Saakashvili was expecting unconditional support from the West, and the West had given him reason to think he would have it', I said. Hundreds of people responded to my article on the *Washington Post* website. 'Why is this conflict being reported in such a one-sided way?' one reader asked. 'Is it possible to make policy on the basis of such one-sided information?' Another reader wondered: 'How can the US be so confused about this reality, lecturing from thousands of miles away, steeped in the twentieth-century politics of ideological confrontation?' This hits the nail on the head.

When dramatic events unfolded in Ukraine at the end of 2013, it became clear that the West had not learned its lesson. Once again, Russia was blamed for everything. Neither the Western media nor political leaders were seriously interested in thoroughly analysing the history and background of the crisis in Crimea.

As a reminder: for the people of my generation, it was incomprehensible that Crimea had been incorporated into the Ukrainian Soviet Socialist Republic in 1954. No one asked the residents of Crimea at the time whether they wanted this transfer from Russia to Ukraine. At least it took place in the context of a common state, the Soviet Union, and it did not have any particular impact on the people's everyday lives. But at the end of 1991, as they hastily tore the Soviet Union apart, the leaders of Russia and Ukraine forgot about the people. Discord was inevitable sooner or later, and when the people of Crimea were finally asked which country they wanted to be citizens of, they answered unequivocally.

Ignoring the will of the people that was expressed in the referendum of March 2014, Western leaders decided to punish Russia and impose sanctions. But sanctions are a weapon that cuts both ways and, furthermore, they cannot influence Russia's position on this matter. Russia is not raising the question of sanctions and is not calling for them to be lifted. However, it is in the interest of the West itself to give up its sanctions policy, because the sanctions have only one effect: increasing mutual alienation, which makes dialogue more difficult.

Russia has vast experience in foreign policy and diplomacy. It is based on a centuries-old history and has been enriched by the achievements of perestroika, which produced outstanding examples of dialogue and constructive cooperation. We did not emerge from the Cold War only to hear the drums of war again.

I do not believe that the collapse of trust over recent years is irreversible. I view it as a lapse, a mistake. Fixing this mistake will take time and patience, common sense and negotiating skills. And, above all, we must understand that we live together on this fragile planet, and we are all responsible for its future fate.

Afterword

I recently met with Carmelo Abela, the Maltese Minister for Foreign Affairs. Abela had arrived in Moscow for negotiations with Russian Foreign Minister Sergei Lavrov and requested that we meet to discuss plans regarding the thirtieth anniversary of my Malta summit talks with US President George H. W. Bush. The Maltese wanted to commemorate this anniversary in a fitting and proper manner. Leaders and diplomats from many countries were invited to the commemorative ceremony.

Our objective, said the minister, is to remind people about this supremely important event. We must underscore its global significance, and we must also give impetus to serious reflections on both the current state of international relations and contemporary challenges that need to be addressed via dialogue and cooperation.

I welcomed this intention.

'And how old were you when those talks took place?' I asked my guest. 'Seventeen', he replied. 'More than old enough to grasp that history was being made before my very eyes.'

Indeed, the summit represented a genuine historical turning point. Even the way it was arranged and conducted possessed a drama and symbolism all its own.

The Americans initially proposed holding the talks aboard warships stationed off the Maltese coast. We agreed. Our ship and its American counterpart were both anchored in a roadstead in anticipation of the meeting. But the night ushered in such a violent storm that there was no way delegation members could board the two vessels. It was a good thing a civilian craft of ours, the *Maxim Gorky*, was in port at the time. We invited George Bush and the American delegation onto the ship, and it was there, aboard a non-military passenger liner, that the summit took place – a turn of events laden with symbolism.

In Malta, the US president and I declared that our respective countries no longer regarded each other as enemies and were ready to develop a cooperative relationship that would in due course become a partnership. We discussed the entire range of problems facing us during that turbulent time. And we agreed on many issues.

Though serious hurdles awaited us after Malta, we managed to continue what we had begun at meetings with US President Ronald Reagan in Geneva and Reykjavik – first and foremost in the area of nuclear arms reduction.

Today, we must above all strive to prevent the destruction of everything we achieved during those years.

It is precisely to this end that I have written the present book. My recent meetings and conversations with politicians, business figures, scholars, journalists and publishers have convinced me that people are tired of feeling they are at a dead end, that global prospects are lacking. As I have been told more than once, today's turbulent world has bewildered people and driven many into the embrace of pessimism and apathy. Many, yes, but I hope by no means all.

When I left the post of president, I did not leave politics altogether. It is true, of course, that throughout these years I have wielded no public power and carried out no official assignments. But I have always believed, and continue to believe, that former leaders should not remain silent, that they have every right to put forward proposals and issue warnings. And in today's situation – one of seeming impasse – it is a matter of duty for experienced, authoritative individuals who have borne the burden of difficult, responsible decision-making to say their piece.

For as long as my health permitted, I was an almost annual participant in the Nobel Peace Laureate Forums. Engaging with other laureates and representatives of Nobel-winning organizations has always been interesting and instructive. We are different in some ways and have our own agendas, but on one thing, at least, we all agree: history's course is not ineluctable, nothing in it is predetermined, and we can all do our part to ensure that its arc tends towards peace, justice and humaneness.

Pessimism, therefore, is no ally of ours. My colleagues have maintained their faith in a better future and human-kind's capacity to shape this future without shrinking from the obstacles and surprises that inevitably arise on our path.

'Walk and ye shall reach.' It is not for nothing that these words, from the ancient Indian Vedas, have entered the languages of the world's peoples. Variations on them can be found in Latin, in the Bible and in classics of world literature.

There is great wisdom in these words. They articulate the conviction that humankind, having learned to negotiate vast expanses, to penetrate the mysteries of the universe, to create innumerable material benefits, can also rise to another, possibly more arduous challenge – that of organizing the global world in a way that would enable all its peoples and individual denizens to live in safety and security, in judicious union with nature, and in accordance with the demands of reason and morality.

Afterword translated by Leo Shtutin